# WARRIORTRADING

## INSIDE THE MIND OF AN
## ELITE CURRENCY TRADER

CLIFFORD **BENNETT**

**WILEY**

John Wiley & Sons, Inc.

Previously published in 2005 by Wrightbooks, an imprint of John Wiley & Sons Australia, Ltd., 33 Park Road, Milton, Qld 4064. First Australian edition © Clifford Bennett 2005.

Published by John Wiley & Sons, Inc., Hoboken, New Jersey

Published simultaneously in Canada

For general information on our other products and services or for technical support, please contact our Customer Care Department within the United States at (800) 762–2974, outside the United States at (317) 572–3993 or fax (317) 572–4002.

Wiley also publishes its books in a variety of electronic formats. Some content that appears in print may not be available in electronic books. For more information about Wiley products, visit our web site at www.wiley.com.

Library of Congress Cataloging-in-Publication Data

Bennett, Clifford, 1959-
  Warrior trading : inside the mind of an elite currency trader / by Clifford Bennett.
    p. cm.—(Wiley trading series)
  ISBN-13: 978-0-471-77224-8 (cloth)
  ISBN-10: 0-471-77224-0 (cloth)
  1. Speculation.   2. Stocks.   3. Investments.   I. Title.   II. Series.
  HG6015.B46 2006
  332.64—dc22

                                                                                        2005031904

Printed in the United States of America

10 9 8 7 6 5 4 3 2 1

**To Ellisa, Ami, and Lucas,**
*three spirits whom I wish to thank for having paid me the greatest compliment and honor by choosing me as their father.
Their inspiration is never-ending.*

**To Tena Panizza,**
*whose belief and love have forever changed my life and set it on a higher course.*

# CONTENTS

# ACKNOWLEDGMENTS

There has never been a book that is an island unto itself, and I would like to thank everyone who has contributed to *Warrior Trading* for their support and assistance.

I'm sure all authors have publishers who contribute significantly to the end result, but I do want to thank Anthony Stone for both his guidance and his patience, and also for recognizing the potential of my original manuscript. I would particularly like to thank Kevin Commins for his steadfast support of the further development and evolution of *Warrior Trading*.

*Know the battlefield terrain; choose your weapon; be the warrior trader.*

### *Be victorious!*

*Financial markets are a battlefield. As in any combat, it is the true warrior who towers above, reaping the fortunes of the vanquished.*

# INTRODUCTION

## REMOVE YOURSELF FROM THE HERD

Among the thousands—perhaps millions—of traders in the world today, there is an elite group who amasses immense fortunes. It is these individuals, and the stories of their wealth and the kinds of lifestyles they enjoy, who inspire millions around the globe to partake in the greatest game on earth: trading in financial markets. These individuals, through focused effort, a constant search for knowledge, immense courage, and concentrated determination, win out over the throngs of lesser traders. They are the warrior traders. After more than 20 years of trading in global financial markets, and chatting and discussing markets with the best warrior traders from New York to Switzerland, I feel privileged to have learned a great deal. I feel even more privileged to now have the opportunity to put down in these pages some of the trading secrets I have discovered.

I say "secrets," but this does not mean the concepts are difficult. Perhaps like the most valuable gifts in life, they are really self-apparent. Yet despite this, they are somehow unseen by the majority. Even those who have discovered some of these secrets usually end up drifting back to their previous, unsuccessful trading styles. In fact, even the best of the warrior traders have to constantly guard themselves against the tendency toward complacency and even arrogance when profits have been growing particularly well for a period. My hope is that the information in these pages will quickly accelerate traders from beginner to warrior status; however, it is important to realize at the outset that this can happen only if warrior status is truly desired. Once arrived at, the new challenge is staying there.

> *The most important warrior secret of all: Your level of success in the world of financial markets is entirely up to you and has nothing to do with what the markets are doing.*

The most important warrior secret of all: Your level of success in the world of financial markets is entirely up to you and has nothing to do with what the markets are doing. There will always be bull markets and bear markets. The occurrence of good or bad luck, if luck exists at all, evens out over time. Great success and the attaining of warrior trader status come about as a result of commitment, a never-ending willingness to learn, steadfast determination, and that rare ingredient, a touch of humility. Throughout the ages, all great warriors have had these same characteristics.

The global financial markets of today are every bit as vicious psychologically, and sometimes even physically, as the battles the great warriors throughout history encountered. To face these markets, or potential battlefields, warrior traders must be strong. Mental toughness is not enough, however. To be a warrior, you must understand the deeper reality of processes that to many may seem simple, yet they are not. The warrior trader must not only be knowledgeable in all areas of market theory, but also specialize in one particular style of battle. This one particular style is that which best suits the specific individual. Warrior traders must also take an individualistic approach to these theories. The subjects of fundamental economics and technical analysis are scrutinized in this book in such a fashion.

The opportunity for immense wealth stems directly from the fundamental reality underlying any market. How you successfully mine for this gold is very different from what you may have read previously. You may never have read or heard of these subjects being depicted in the manner in which they are here. Some may even think my views are a little brutal, but such is the nature of the battlefield. My aim is to shed light on those whom you will undoubtedly find yourself pitted against on the trading floor and more often now in the faceless and perhaps even more ruthless environment of the electronic marketplace. Approach these subjects with an open mind, and the pennies will begin to drop—at first slowly and then by the truckload. This experience is, I believe, within everyone's reach, but only if they are really prepared to make the effort, to make the journey, both inward and outward.

Almost by definition, a warrior trader attacks markets in a very different way from the rest of the market participants. This is obvious when you think about it—those who are financially enriched beyond what most people can only dream of will naturally behave differently from the majority in their arena of choice. Their different behavior allows them to scoop the wealth of everyone else involved. The reason they can keep doing this year in, year out is that the rest of the participants in the market rarely learn the lessons offered. The market is a great and extremely rapid teacher, if only we are willing to listen. In each and every loss, as well as in each and every win, there are powerful lessons to be learned. Most market participants believe they are approaching the game in a winning way; that losses are the result of bad luck; that, at most, a small amount of fine-tuning is required in their approach. In the worst-case scenario, some will maintain the ridiculous and odd belief that it was the market that was wrong. The market at large, often described as the "herd" or the "crowd," never takes the time to step back and consider whether its entire approach to the process might be inappropriate. Reading the same textbooks and coming to a relatively uniform understanding of the market, the herd never believes that it could be blinding itself. However, the methodology being so enthusiastically explored and developed by almost all market participants is actually fundamentally flawed. What is different about warrior traders is that they know this—and they seek to use this knowledge to ruthlessly take advantage of the opportunity presented.

*The good news, however, is that anyone who is prepared to open his or her mind to a different perspective of world markets and work assiduously to perfect the art of trading can indeed become a member of this elite group. You can become a warrior trader.*

Most losing and break-even market participants never consider throwing their entire approach into the rubbish bin where it belongs. This is, in essence, why warrior traders are able to continue to harvest enormous wealth, year after year, from the rest of the market—the roll-up of market losers just continues. The good news, however, is that anyone who is prepared to open his or her mind to a different perspective of world markets and work assiduously to perfect the art of trading can indeed become a member of this elite group. You can become a warrior trader.

The purpose here, then, is to introduce you to some fresh and different perspectives regarding markets, looking at fundamental and technical analysis, as well as to provoke a discovery of how best to interact and trade with a market as an individual. Some broadly accepted textbook principles will be turned on their heads as we embark on a journey to the core of markets. An enormous number of books and seminars are available on the subject of trading and investing on the share market, and most tend to generalize about what markets "should" do. This book is about discovering and understanding how markets actually operate in the real world and learning how to trade not just to make a living but to possibly make a fortune—time and time again.

Even at this stage of the book, you may be starting to see that this makes perfect sense. If mainstream market theorists were on the ball and correct most of the time, there would not be the opportunity for a select few to repeatedly snatch away the chips placed in the market by others. If a person could simply read a book or follow the step-by-step rules of an acknowledged expert to be assured of market success, everybody would do so. In fact, something very different from the arguments of most market theorists is happening in markets, as will be discussed throughout this book. In order to gain the most benefit from this discussion, it is important to approach it with an open mind.

However, be warned: It will not be easy to attain this status nor is it simply a matter of following a step-by-step guide. This book will take you on a journey through the characteristics, the knowledge and skills, and the psychological and even Zen-like state required of the true warrior trader. Warrior trading is about the harmonious intersection of oneself with the battleground; it is about knowing exactly where you stand in the market and having the ability to see 360 degrees around you, absorbing everything that is happening and acting to take full advantage of any situation that presents itself.

Markets are very similar to warfare. Just as the warriors of old rode out to battle with the confidence and knowledge to conquer new lands and foes, so do the warriors of the market thrive on the battleground of the trading floor.

## MY JOURNEY TO WARRIOR TRADER STATUS

Perhaps you're wondering what it is that gives me the right to write this book and instruct you in the techniques used by warrior traders. I have been trading in markets the world over for more than 20 years. My first profession was the navy. I was a junior officer in the Royal Australian Navy when I realized I would rather be at the center of things than on the outside protecting what really mattered. I did not know it at the time, but I was swapping one form of warrior for another. The mentality required in the war room of a destroyer is not that different from that required to trade in modern markets. There is a lot of information pouring in very quickly from an array of sources and computer screens, but it all comes to a 50–50 decision—shoot or not, buy or sell—and the results of your decision are known all too quickly.

My own path through the financial markets of the world has incorporated commodity markets, equity markets, and, in the main, the global currency markets. Foreign exchange is still one of the fastest-growing markets in the world, and is overwhelming the largest financial market in the world. Trading in foreign exchange markets is a great vantage point from which to perceive the forests of other markets and the major trends within them, which are increasingly tightly linked. It is well worth noting the stong trend today toward the greater interdependence of markets. By this I mean that fluctuations in oil, for instance, can affect the U.S. dollar's value as well as equity and other markets.

Starting out at the local Australian investment bank Macquarie Bank, I set forth on a journey that would have me traveling the world for some of the top global investment banks, trading in most markets and advising some of the world's largest institutions—from Coca-Cola to central banks—on their foreign exchange exposure.

Over the years, I have called some great currency market, equity market, interest rate market, and gold market rallies, and equally called some of the greatest bear trends in these markets. I have traded my own money in the futures pits and traded the tens of millions of dollars placed under my auspices by global investment banks. When central banks have been intervening in markets, I have sold against them and won enormous sums. On other occasions, I have lost. But it is the ability to learn from both experiences, and not just celebrate the one and mourn the other, that, I believe, separates warrior traders from the herd of other market participants.

At the end of 2004, my independent currency forecasting and advisory firm, FxMax, which advises several banks and a host of clients all around the world, won the prestigious Bloomberg Global FX Survey. The award was for forecasting, before most even imagined the possibility, a major collapse in the U.S. dollar.

Interestingly, when I spoke at the 2004 Euromoney Foreign Exchange Conference in London early in the year, I became involved in a debate with a member of President George W. Bush's economic team. At the time, the Bush administration was decidedly bullish about its currency, though the mantra later changed to allowing the dollar to slide. Still, the bullish U.S. dollar argument by this individual was based on the simple assumption that the United States was the greatest entrepreneurial nation on earth and, in their assessment, would always continue to draw in huge capital flows and therefore maintain a strong currency. However, as I was quick to point out at the time, the real world of human emotion is not as simple as that.

As comprehensive as the Harvard and other business schools of the world are, the decisions of businesspeople and traders around the world always end up being subjective and emotional, whether they acknowledge it or not and whether they like it or not.

It is this warrior insight that can allow you to outperform the people presumed to be the most "in the know" in the world and, likewise, the largest institutions in the world—as I have with my firm.

The fact that a small, independent firm in Sydney can outperform the largest and most successful investment banks in the world, and by a large margin, only highlights that success in the markets is about taking the warrior path and not just, as many assume, about the sheer size of the combatant.

## THE VALUE OF WARRIOR TRADING

A lot of people question the value to the community of being involved in financial markets, especially when that role is sometimes—or even all the time—speculating purely for profit. However, it is the participants in a market, those willing to walk on the field of financial battle, who create and reinforce those very markets. Markets ensure that resources are distributed to the most productive endeavors in the most efficient way. The everyday lives of all the members of a community are enhanced by markets, be they the local fruit and vegetable market or the New York Stock Exchange. The improvement in the quality of life for an increasing number of people around the world, albeit imperfectly at times, is due to the explosion in global trade over the last two to three decades, which is entirely due to the operation and support of efficient global financial markets. The more liquid a market is, the greater the volume of activity, the more efficient it is, therefore providing the greatest benefit. Traders add tremendous liquidity, thereby creating far more efficient markets than could otherwise be the case, for everyone.

It has been an honor to participate in these markets for over two decades and to have met some truly inspiring individuals. Some of these individuals are genuinely wealthy, to a degree beyond the comprehension of most of us. Because of the contribution to our local and global communities that the many different market participants make, striving to speculate successfully in financial markets is a noble cause. Out of this noble pursuit rise but a few legends, and these are the warrior traders.

## IS IT ALL A GAME?

I have seen people manage markets extremely well—such that, although they frequently lose, they always trend to greater and greater profits. However, I have more often witnessed poor management of business exposure or speculative pursuits, and this has often led to companies being forced to lay off a large number of employees, resulting in the ruin of some individuals. Trading in financial markets is a very real activity indeed, with sometimes serious consequences, and one should not allow the advent of the Internet and online trading, which can be viewed positively for a number of reasons, to lead one to think it is a simple, no-pain game.

A game it is, but a dangerous and challenging one that is extremely complex and for which there is no get-rich-quick scheme. For those who are willing, I believe there is a path to great wealth in financial markets. From my own experience, and that of several emphatically successful traders, I regard that path as a timeless one. It has existed throughout the ages and is most closely associated with the path of great warriors.

I trust this book helps guide you to the prosperous discovery of a greater knowledge and awareness of your own self through the process of trading in financial markets, for there is a true warrior in each of us. Trading in markets is a noble discipline and assuredly has its rightful place in our modern society. It is certainly a challenging pursuit, and in the face of immense challenge we have the opportunity to find our true strength, if we are willing to dig for it and therefore discover tremendous fulfillment on many levels, including financial.

First, warrior traders have to do their homework, develop a specific technique of battle attuned to their natural strengths, and survey the terrain. Then they must continually fight with all their strength and expertise.

From where I sit, there will always be a minority who succeed beyond the bounds of most people's imaginings of wild success, and a majority who toil and sweat for little if any return.

*Know the terrain, choose your weapon, be the warrior trader.*

Clifford Bennett
Sydney, Australia
Winter 2005

# PART I

# WARRIOR HOMEWORK

# CHAPTER 1

# WARRIOR FUNDAMENTAL ANALYSIS

Fundamental analysis is the consideration and study of all economic and political factors that may have an impact on a particular market. For an individual stock, such a factor may be the development of a specific technology. For a currency, the fundamental factors are the more macroeconomic forces at play in the host currency economy and relative to other economies.

A great example of the power of fundamental forces and the frequent misunderstanding or, worse, excited misinterpretation of them can be found in the movements in the equity, bond, and currency markets of early 2004 that resulted from some comments made by the chairman of the U.S. Federal Reserve, Alan Greenspan. Interest rate hikes in the United States were at that time widely expected, and expected to continue through the year. Although the market was a little unsure of the amount by which they would be increased, the consensus seemed to be that rates would rise gradually. Indeed, this was what the chairman had told markets previously.

The excitement came when Chairman Greenspan made a simple remark: that if inflation turned up sharply, the U.S. central bank would have to raise rates aggressively in response. However, he also stated that this was not the expectation. The theorists and writers behind virtually all the fundamental research reports from the major investment banks and brokers around the world suddenly became excited about rates being raised "aggressively" in the United States. Equities went south at a great rate, as did bond markets, and the U.S. dollar rallied sharply. Above the din of clamoring commentaries about the intended aggressive rate hikes, I felt like a lone wolf calling out in the wilderness as I maintained that nothing had changed and these market shifts would quickly reverse. All that Chairman Greenspan had done was state the obvious. It is Central Bank Behavior 101: If inflation becomes rampant, central banks respond by raising rates aggressively.

Did the chairman expect inflation to be rampant? No, quite the contrary. Did the chairman expect to be raising rates aggressively? No. Chairman Greenspan simply stated that the Federal Reserve would respond appropriately if economic conditions were different from what they were forecast to be, which was ongoing low or benign inflation.

A few days later, Chairman Greenspan was forced to reiterate to mistakenly excited markets that inflation was not expected to be a problem and rates would most likely be raised at a measured pace. Of course, the markets did indeed reverse after this announcement. A great deal of volatility in the market and pain for the majority of traders and investors had resulted from a false perception of the true fundamental reality. It is easy to get excited and run with the herd. It is far more profitable to seek out the true fundamentals—the warrior fundamentals.

## THE REAL ECONOMIC FUNDAMENTAL FORCES THAT HAVE AN IMPACT ON MARKETS

There are two important points to remember when looking at the fundamental forces that have an impact on markets. First, the real fundamental driving forces of any market are rarely described by the latest economic releases. Neither can they be comprehended though the regular diatribes of additional spin placed on them by the majority of market commentators.

Second, the economics of a country are a very different animal from the economics of a particular market, just as the economics of a company are entirely separate from the movements of its share price.

Some companies can increase sales during a slowing in the broader economy just as they can in an expanding economy. Of course, expanding sales do not necessarily mean a higher stock price. It really does get complicated. We must always remember that all pricing models for stocks, and all economic theories, are attempts to simplify what is, in reality, complex by nature. Therefore, every such theory is by definition in error. Such theories are useful as a starting point for understanding the processes in play, but should not be taken as providing the answer. This flies in the face of what we all want to believe and seek to find. It is the strength to accept the reality that contributes to the achieving of warrior trading status. Warrior traders know that almost anything can happen in a market at any time, because in truth almost no one really understands what is going on despite the detail of their analysis. In the end, of course, it is simply the movement of price of a stock and not the competence of the board that determines whether you as a trader make a profit or a loss. Understanding one does not necessarily lead to the other, despite the apparent connection.

*Finding the real fundamental forces that drive any market, as opposed to what the broader market crowd perceives the fundamental forces to be, requires the warrior trader to stand back from the crowd, to keep it simple and keep it human.*

Finding the real fundamental forces that drive any market, as opposed to what the broader market crowd perceives the fundamental forces to be, requires the warrior trader to stand back from the crowd, to keep it simple and keep it human. Sometimes basic common sense can cut through a highly technical and complex argument to the core of the real issue.

One quick way of standing back from the crowd, of course, is to find a good, real-world, down-to-earth economist or analyst and discuss the issues in some detail—not one who sounds clever, but one who gets it right in a consistent fashion. This is, perhaps, easier said than done, however. As a general rule, economists do not publish their complete track records, and there is usually a very good reason for this. No doubt, all will lay claim to great calls of the past as they attempt to justify their economic credibility. But in truth, anyone could do this. Make enough forecasts, and you are bound to get some right.

I can similarly lay claim to some great financial market forecasts—some over many years; others over shorter periods. But these would represent just a handful of the forecasts I have made over many years. A few of my forecasts were badly wrong—although I like to think they were corrected quickly enough to prevent any significant damage. The task of predicting market movements is a subjective process, however, and if ever there was a group with subjective memory skills, it is economists. These days, I have my own independent research firm, FxMax (www.fxmax.com), and I am able to provide a quantified track record of my forecasting performance—indeed, it is a record that I see as crucial to my firm's success.

When it comes to the predictions of many banks and financial institutions, however, I believe that their motives are necessarily compromised. Even if a leading market economist with a major investment bank or institution wanted to and even if the economist's predictions had been successful in the past, it is unlikely that the bank or institution would want to risk the credibility of its brand name on the track record of the average economist. The truth is that the research produced by the major financial market economists is for marketing purposes only. The main objective of all the commentary and predictive suggestion is to get clients trading. Whether the research was correct or not does not affect the profitability of the bank or broker, as long as the research generated interest and trading activity among clients.

Figure 1.1 shows the forecasts published in the major Australian daily newspaper *The Age* as part of its economic survey, which included currency forecasts for the $US/$AUD over a 6- to 12-month period. These forecasts are collected from around 20 different banks, brokers, and financial institutions, as well as from university and economic-policy groups. What is most striking about the forecasts is their inaccuracy.

It is a similar story in all markets around the world. Markets are tough to forecast, especially if forecasts tend to be extrapolations of recent market behavior, which is in the main what they are. It is a very interesting phenomenon that the large majority of market research produced trends, on a daily, weekly, and even monthly basis, to follow the direction of the market. As I mentioned before, it is more accurate to say that research reports tend to be led by market movement rather than preempting it.

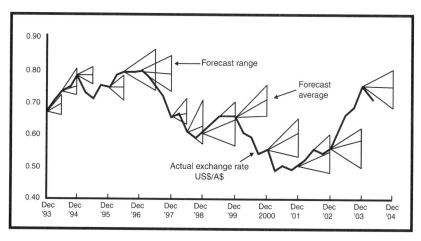

**FIGURE 1.1** Currency Forecasts versus Actual (*Source:* Phillip Spry Bailey, *Mastering Foreign Exchange,* Wrightbooks, 2004.)

One standing joke among most traders and salespeople in the leading institutions is how brokerages or bank economists/strategists have a draw on either side of their desks. On one side are all the fundamental and technical reasons for a bull market. On the other side of the desk are all the fundamental and technical reasons for a bear market. Each morning as these economists/strategists sit down at their desks to write the day's market commentary, they first look to see whether the market is up or down and then reach for the appropriate draw.

Nevertheless, I believe that if you search hard for market economists who, although they are often out of line with the consensus view of their colleagues, over a period of time show a penchant for getting the market right in a regular fashion, you may just find some truly golden information and forecasts. Real-world economists who use common sense and look out the window to consider the world as it is, rather than purely focusing on textbook theories about how it should be, do exist.

However, it is not simply a matter of my suggesting the names of particularly good economists that I listen to and take notice of. As you know, my area of expertise is foreign exchange, so if I were to give you the name of an excellent French economist who understands the European economy to a very fine degree, it would not help you invest in shares on the NYSE. Even if this was your interest, it should not be assumed that you would read and interpret the same economist in the same manner as I would. Some of my clients who have been with me for a long time have come to be able to read between the lines, as it were. They can sense when I am less confident or overconfident. They can sense, perhaps before I do, that I am being stubborn about a view.

What you do need is the will to listen and read widely, and to critically analyze the forecasts of various economists and understand the motivations behind their predictions. Ultimately, this will lead you to those whose voices ring truest in the market, not those who simply talk because a journalist has asked them a question or write because a monthly review is due. Believe me, there is a lot of money to be made from picking the occasions when the consensus is utterly wrong and when the markets have to reverse direction completely. These moments often generate the more significant price movements and lasting trends. It is only real-world market economists who can alert you to such opportunities.

One of my favorite axioms and beliefs about markets is that the most money is to be made when the consensus is wrong. If you think about it, this makes perfect sense. If the consensus view is proven correct by the next batch of data, then the market will move perhaps a little further in that direction. The movement is invariably less than the market hoped for. This is because everyone who believed in that view of that market had already invested accordingly. One does not wait until after an announcement that one believes will be bullish to buy. You buy now in an attempt to get ahead of the crowd. Well, so does everyone else, and if it is the consensus view, then most market participants will have done so. What everyone doing this does not realize is that they now, like everyone else, have in fact become sellers. Their next action in the market will be to sell after the expected resultant rally. The vast majority of market participants are potential sellers, not buyers, on the good news, should it be as they expect. So when the good news comes out as expected, the level of potential buying interest is not all that great; therefore, the price may move up only a little if at all. What happens if the news is not as expected? Then all the potential sellers attempt to sell all at once. The market movement to the downside will be sudden and dramatic.

As I have said, fundamentals drive markets, there is no doubt about that, and one of those fundamentals is market positioning. We will discuss this in greater detail in a later chapter.

## THE REALITY OF FUNDAMENTAL ECONOMICS

Why is economics—that is, the understanding of the real fundamentals that drive and motivate markets—such a challenge? It is because people make up both economies and companies.

"Ah, but economics is about rules, such as the law of diminishing returns, efficient market theory, and portfolio theory," you may say. Well, yes and no. Such so-called laws are merely attempts to generalize about patterns of economic activity that have arisen in the past. But people are emotional, and they also learn and evolve. Therefore, patterns of behavior alter and evolve in an organic fashion. It would require a perfect understanding of the motivation and thinking of people in today's society to make a fully accurate assessment and forecast of an economy. Rather a daunting task, I would suggest. Hence, the natural inclination to oversimplify—which is all very well as long as we recognize this process for what it is so that we can see the opportunity from a trading perspective that is then created.

### Reductionist Theory and the Reality of Fundamental Economics

Today's markets are complex, to say the least. Some of the people who make up an economy are also directly involved in markets (all are indirectly involved), and the level of participation in markets is at a historical high. All participants in a market affect that market's price action, and as participation is higher than ever and patterns of behavior continue to evolve, new patterns of economic behavior and market price action are also continually emerging.

Hence, the study of one aspect of this complexity—economic activity data—is simply not enough. Economic data are historical and therefore backward looking by definition. While such data undoubtedly give clues to the likely forward path, they do not represent the future at all. As such, any analysis locked too

WARRIOR FUNDAMENTAL ANALYSIS

tightly into such a perspective cannot succeed. This is why the practitioners of pure economic theory applied to the latest run of data typically have a modest forecasting record. Yet this is precisely the form of analysis that tends to dominate all media reporting on fundamental developments and drive the consensus view. Most economic models are useful in polite conversation, but they cannot compete with the cut and thrust of market realities.

*Economic data are historical and therefore backward looking by definition. While such data undoubtedly give clues to the likely forward path, they do not represent the future at all.*

Indeed, this is not just a theoretical affliction facing the economic world. Quantum physics has demonstrated that reductionist philosophy—that is, the idea of reducing any subject of study to its smallest constituent components—is flawed. For instance, Einstein's theory of relativity works most of the time but not all of the time, and at some levels not at all. Such attempts will ultimately lead to a severe disconnect between expectations and actual events, as the reasoning deduced from the model conflicts with the reality of that future.

Let me explain. As discussed, it is people who make up the economy, not numbers. The confusion among contemporary economists on almost any aspect of any economy is due to the arguably flawed nature of current economic theory. All contemporary economists are schooled in an approach to the subject that is essentially derived from scientific method. This theory is reductionist philosophy. Essentially, this is a means of understanding whereby, when looking at competing theories or explanations for a phenomenon, it is the simplest theory that should be selected. The predominant approach to a subject is then to break it down, reduce the subject to the smallest possible components, and so derive a greater understanding of the subject and a concrete mathematical model to explain it—all in the belief that there is a model that explains what is going on. The reality of markets is that no such model exists. Scary perhaps, but true nonetheless. The warrior trader's willing acceptance of this point allows him or her to respond to fresh developments in a market away from the consensus view more rapidly than other participants, and even to prepare an attack strategy in advance.

The reductionist method is commonly used for predictions and forecasting, based on the explanations derived from prior happenings. Its emphasis is basically on a microscopic approach to understanding, looking to derive a general understanding from the features of a particular.

As the advantages of reductionist philosophy, which certainly greatly accelerated scientific advances in the initial phases, dawned on people, its use quickly spread to the humanities. However, perhaps it is now being too widely applied.

The introduction of this philosophy and methodology of explaining reality (or the *micro*) in terms of a reasoning derived from specific and largely isolated theories diverted attention away from some home truths that quantum physicists, in whose field reductionist philosophy has been used most successfully, are increasingly recognizing. In our complex market reality, all things are connected and cannot be successfully approached in isolation. This is exactly what almost all economic theories that have been taught for decades do. They focus on one particular aspect of economic or fundamental behavior in isolation. They then perceive and prove a degree of correlation with another aspect. This is not the full picture of what is going on, however, and a strict adherence to a particular economic principle will only end in market trading losses.

Further, once a subject is exposed to thought and discussion, its behavior is altered by that very analysis. Any group of human beings who begin to question themselves, in particular, why they respond in a certain way to a particular set of events is unlikely to respond in the same way in the future once the self-examination has occurred.

Such is also the case in the field of economics, and particularly so when looking at financial markets. Economic theorists striving to understand, in greater and greater detail, the various machinations of modern economies have accomplished only one thing: the sleight-of-hand skill that seemingly enables historically constructed models to follow an economy or market with such rapidity that they seem to be keeping pace with real-world developments—or even to be forward looking. This is not actually the case, however, despite the mass false impression that is achieved through the use of modern communication technology to quickly analyze and explain real-time events. Rarely does such analysis *lead* the real-time event, however—a subtle yet awakening distinction that few market participants seem to recognize.

Almost all economic analysis and market analysis of an event that is distributed to the clients of all the banks and brokerage houses the world over is actually in hindsight. It therefore can only come across to the reader as being particularly accurate and insightful in nature. These qualities impress the reader and give the individual confidence in dealing with that bank or broker when trading in these markets. In fact, it is often the case that the research produced is so perfectly formatted, presented, in-depth, and generally impressive that many clients believe it gives them an advantage over other traders and will do almost anything to get that research. Such research has its place in providing the warrior with a broad knowledge of what has occurred recently and historically, but the warrior does not make the mistake of interpreting such analysis as in any way an accurate forecast of the future. There are three main types of human creatures in banks and brokerage dealing rooms: economists/researchers, traders, and salespeople. There is one distinction the managers of such organizations never forget, unless to their peril. That is to keep researchers away from trading, and traders away from research. They are different activities. One is backward looking; one is forward looking. It is important not to confuse the two perspectives. Market *view* and *trading* are two distinct activities. This is one of the golden nuggets of wisdom possessed by warrior traders.

## People and the Reality of Fundamental Economics

As mentioned, the tremendous exposure to and involvement with financial markets by everyday people—their analysis and future probability—impact the economic decisions of those very people. Whereas a decade ago a cut in interest rates would have sounded like good news to the public, simply generating Pavlov dog–like response of increased borrowing and spending, an interest rate cut today may have the entirely opposite effect. The general public may reduce spending as it is alerted to potential economic risks that lie ahead. However, interest rate increases can generate a sense that people "better get that house and car and lock in the loan rates before they go even higher." So consumption can, on occasion, actually increase after an interest rate hike. It is a complex world.

Even the physical sciences are beginning to recognize that everything is an art. $E = MC^2$? Well, almost, most of the time, but not, in fact, always, according to more recent discoveries in quantum physics. As you will learn throughout the pages of this book, any field of study that involves human beings is an art. Economies are very much about people; therefore, economics as a discipline of understanding is an art. As an art, individual interpretation naturally abounds, and therein lies the opportunity to find a valuable real-world economist in your market.

The argument about the reliability of contemporary economic thought can, in a way, be cut short by the simple recognition that even economists trained in the same school will have a different take on which way an economy or market is headed. Economics really is a very subjective art form. But to tear it down is not to contribute to the financial success of our trading, other than its value in helping us to recognize that the process is flawed and therefore may of itself create opportunities in the pricing of markets.

## The Failings of Fundamental Economics

An approach to markets based on contemporary economic principles and the predictions or writings of those who follow such arguments is, therefore, unlikely to lead to any great financial success, for two main reasons:

1. The analysis provided may well be based on flawed economic principles in the first place.
2. The analysis provided is subject to, and influenced by, market movement itself. Warrior traders recognize that it is often the recent direction of the price movement that drives the tone of the fundamental research provided by the major houses, rather than the other way around, as they would have us believe.

Ultimately, objectivity is lost.

This is not to say that all market commentaries should be ignored—there are some excellent examples of winning research writers out there. You have to do some mining to find these diamonds, however. One cannot assume that just because the bank or house name is impressive and distinguished the research will be right more often than it is wrong, and good research needs to do just that and in a manner that encourages profitable trading activity. These winning research writers tend not to be mainstream, preferring instead to utilize additional principles in deriving their market view. The mainstream commentaries have value in providing a guide as to how most of the market is thinking (or will be thinking). They remain a force to be reckoned with, and, indeed, no trend will be sustained without this contributing activity—albeit, usually in the middle or toward the end of a trend, as the crowd catches up and the arguments begin to be justified and revised.

Further, there is a significant time delay between an event on the ground, such as a shift in consumer purchasing or an over-run in production, and that event becoming apparent in the released data stream. In most cases, the data can lag by three or more months. This time lag is so significant that, although surprises in economic data may already have corrected themselves at ground level, the discussions of what was happening months ago—an aberration—may still be in progress. Broad consensus views can therefore be far behind reality.

Some would argue that the current data stream is the best we have to work with and, therefore, that is how we should proceed. The problem is that the market generally has no true comprehension of this data-reality gap, and therefore makes assumptions based on data that have a far greater variability than is initially recognized. This means that if you rely on economic data for a view on an economy, or a market, you are working with dated tools.

Admittedly, this is an overly simplistic description of the enormous and deservedly respected art of economics, but it is done to make a point. There are quite capable economists out there who lift their eyes from the textbooks and data in an effort to get an understanding of what is happening in real time, but they are in the minority. It can be difficult for them to be heard. They are often shouted down by the economist masses who think of their university textbook as a bible and tend to sing in unison, thus drowning some of the more talented independent voices.

To my mind, the majority of economists are like meteorologists who don't look out the window. If they are heavily absorbed in the stream of data and charts on their desks, using proven techniques of reasonable success rates in deriving future weather patterns that enable a forecast, but they fail to look out the window as they put pen to paper, then they risk getting it very wrong indeed. If the meteorologist says, "It is going to be raining heavily for most of the day," and then you, yourself, look out to see that the skies are clear, do you grab your umbrella if you are only going for a short walk? No. Why then do so many traders staunchly follow the market forecasts of economists who are operating in an environment that is essentially art rather than science? Because most traders just read the research presented to them on a daily basis without bothering to look out the window for themselves. Warrior traders sit on the roof and get a feel for the real-world environment for themselves, as well as absorbing the commentaries of proven market artisans.

## REAL FUNDAMENTAL FACTORS

There are unquestionably real fundamental forces that do drive financial markets. Looking at the data and perceiving the real fundamental forces behind what is actually happening are two distinct fields of endeavor, however. They can be successfully married only if the practitioner is mindful of the shortcomings inherent in the data.

*No doubt about it, on a macro level, markets move because of fundamental forces acting on them.*

In applying real fundamentals, opportunities abound for those who question and observe in equal amounts. No doubt about it, on a macro level, markets move because of fundamental forces acting on them. All major trends are the result of a significant shift in fundamental forces to a new paradigm or an expansion of a previous state of affairs. If there

19

is a fundamental shock, such as a terrorist attack or major natural disaster, the price shift can be dramatic and sharp.

Additionally, if there is no apparent shift in the fundamentals, the markets can still shift dramatically—although perhaps more gradually. This is because the fundamental forces that cause such movements are a consistent influence. When it comes to considering price action and the work of fundamental forces, I imagine these influencing factors to be similar to the forces that act on the water that is stored in a dam during a period of low water usage. While little or no water may be leaving the dam, water continues to trickle into it. Even though there may have been little price movement for a period of time, it is not the case that the fundamental forces have been dormant. The underlying fundamental forces are always still at work. The pressure has been quietly building, and almost anything can now act as a catalyst for its release.

Apart from the economic fundamental forces at work upon a market, there are several other large factors that dictate the direction of our markets. The first of these is emotion, which is addressed in the next section. Alongside the weight of fundamental forces and emotion that daily have an impact on price action are two other major forces: the media and the enormous size of modern-day capital flows.

The conveyance of market information instantaneously via the media reduces the opportunity for objective individual assessment to play its role. The influence of the media is most strongly seen in what is commonly known as the *front-page effect*. The essence of this principle is that once a market movement hits the front page of a standard daily newspaper, the unfurling of the market trend being discussed in that story is complete and it is time to go the other way. In other words, once a market shift has become significant enough to make it to the front page, it has effectively been recognized by all market participants, and they will have positioned themselves appropriately. All those who want to act have done so. There is only the market crowd who are still coming to terms with the news, and it is these Johnny-come-latelies who, last of all, react to the front-page story. The warrior traders, lying in wait for the gullible crowd, have learned that this situation often represents the last wave of liquidity in which to reverse their winning positions and realize those paper profits.

There is at least one warrior trader of whom I have heard who sits in the Swiss Alps most of the year and trades only when markets hit the front page. A quite important aspect of markets that needs to be recognized is that they evolve, and characteristics can shift and change somewhat. For instance, most markets are traded far more heavily today by less professional traders—that is, traders who do not work for large institutions and are focused more on the big picture such as fund managers, but traders who are in the market for the money they can make today. The day traders tend to react to a greater degree and follow media headlines in a herdlike fashion more than the larger institutions. This is not because the large institutions are more clever—far from it. It is a simple function of the role of committees (as discussed later) in large institutions, which slow down their trading response time. Ten years ago one could sell a bull market that had just hit the front page the very next day and do reasonably well. In today's market, it is often best to wait at least three days, and perhaps longer, for everyone who is going to react to the front-page story to finally do so. The principle remains the same, but the market has evolved to be a slightly different animal, and so your trading response has to evolve as well.

The second of these major influences—the enormous capital that is endlessly flowing into stock markets—also provides for a slight variation to the front-page effect theory, which I refer to as the "no doorway is big enough" phenomenon. This situation has come about as a result of the global shift toward private superannuation that has swept the world during the past 20 years or so. This shift has generated huge parcels of money that continually move around the globe to different markets. Overall, these movements are largely dependent on sentiment and beliefs and rarely have anything to do with reality. They are part of investment or pension funds that are compelled by their investment principles to head into equity, bond, or property markets within a particular country. At other times they are simple currency plays with no other purpose beyond speculation.

While with the front-page effect it is imperative to lead the market and then exit quickly as the situation begins to reinforce itself, one interesting aspect of the huge capital tanks that continue to pour money into the market is that if you get into a trend early, you do not always have to look to get out early, as was once the case. It can take quite a period of time for the now-massive herd of very large players to shuffle through the sometimes still relatively narrow market gateway—leaving plenty of time for the nimble warrior to slip through.

The challenge for warrior traders is to escape the pure application of orthodox economic theory and tread a lesser-known path toward theories of varied principles that may exist in the future, based on a study of broad sociological shifts currently taking place. Clearly, some economists already do this, but it would be preferable for it to be the mainstream, centrist approach of contemporary economic thought.

## HOW WARRIOR TRADERS CAN USE REAL FUNDAMENTAL FORCES

If a market goes up, the majority of analysts present the arguments for a bull market. If a market goes down, the analysts present the reasons for a bear market. It is rarely the other way round—that is, analysts will rarely present reasons for a bear market when the market goes up, and vice versa. Economics, as it is commonly taught, is a market-following discipline, not a market-leading one.

Certainly, there is much prognostication about the direction of a market, but such predictions are so often incorrect that their originators barely notice the error. By the next day or month, as the market moves differently from the forecast, one can typically find the analysts busy writing papers on why the market did so and how it makes perfect sense after all.

This paradigm leaves a market wide open for successful speculation. This is a fortunate situation for the few warrior traders. While the majority of participants are enjoying their grand feeling of intellectual acceptance among their peers, justifying this with a lengthy dissection of the so-called relevant economic variables, it is often the case that successful speculators have already acted on a different scenario—after which these warrior traders simply wait for the broader market to catch up. The risk/reward of such an approach favors the warrior spectacularly.

There is no doubt the market is driven by the real fundamental forces acting on it. But there is a crucial distinction between the majority of traders and warrior traders, and there is a reason why the market crowd gets it wrong so many times: What the speculators do is accelerate the market in the direction of the net real fundamental forces. Indeed, price movements in the direction of the real fundamentals are always very fast and rewarding. These successful warrior traders take over, using real fundamental expectations. They also know only too well yet another important truth about markets: They always overshoot. So if one gets positioned into a fundamentally driven trend early, the warrior reaps the benefit of having had the fundamental insight early and of the overshoot phase, which he or she will be able to grasp as such in real time. The very aggressive warriors will also look to make a profit on the correction to the overshoot, which itself will be exaggerated. After that, the market will tend to narrow in range but in a very random manner. Most warriors play golf during this phase of a big price shift. But getting back to the lack of market understanding of the real fundamentals.

You're probably thinking, "How is this possible? There is an objective reality as to the state of the economy or economies that can be ascertained and then constructed so as to understand what it is that drives the markets." Although this is partly accurate, the true nature of any economy is completely unknown in real time. Weekly and monthly fluctuations due to natural disasters or the political instability that comes with wars, and a great many other variables, leave economists waiting for the more reliable quarterly data. And yet, even at the monthly level of activity, the data that economists work from will lag significantly behind reality as a result of the time difference between collection and publication. This time lag means that September data sometimes do not appear until early November. Ultimately, then, economists are left dealing with only what they have in front of them: historical, backward-looking data.

Meanwhile, in real time, the market is moving, invariably taking a punt on how future data will unfold. And who is it that leads the market? As you might have guessed, it is the warrior speculators. Just as such individuals would have led the masses into battle in previous ages, orchestrating the terms of the contest and preparing the ground, so too do these latter-day warriors lead the market crowd onward, only to take advantage of their position as the thundering hordes seek to climb aboard the next directional wave.

But why is it that the successful warrior speculators lead the way? Primarily, it is because they are of a different mentality. They think more quickly and act more decisively. They do so because what they want out of the market is not so much to be smarter but to be faster, for they recognize that this is how they get paid. Positioning themselves to get maximum gain from market movements requires that they be there before anyone else and know which way the market will turn. Thus, a vital skill required by warrior traders is speed of decision.

The market economists, however, are thorough and cautious in their analysis and consider both sides of the argument, bull versus bear, repeatedly. This leaves those same market economists open to argument and persuasion. The greater your study of economies, the greater your vulnerability to persuasion. The situation arises purely because economies are so complex, and the perception of them is made ever more complex than even the objective reality because of the impact of a host of theoretical positions, such as reductionist philosophy. There are always many valid bullish and bearish fundamental arguments to be made about any economy at any point of time. But all of this ignores the simple fact that in the midst of this chaotic onslaught of the observation of variables and theoretical application, there perennially exists a subtle, covert, and persuasive force—the movement of the market itself.

*Warrior traders, then, for the most part view the broad consensus that too often dominates economic outlooks to be, dare I say, fundamentally flawed. But rather than simply deriding this error, the warrior seeks to turn an opponent's weakness into a decisive advantage. Herein exists significant opportunity for those prepared to take up the challenge . . .*

Warrior traders, then, for the most part view the broad consensus that too often dominates economic outlooks to be, dare I say, fundamentally flawed. But rather than simply deriding this error, the warrior seeks to turn an opponent's weakness into a decisive advantage. Herein exists significant opportunity for those prepared to take up the challenge—providing, of course, that one does not fall under the influence of the consensus avalanche of argument.

It is absolutely crucial to successful trading in all markets to understand that economics is an art rather than a science, and that good, real-world economists are probably still in the minority. The warrior has to search for positive track records among analysts and not be blinded into accepting without critique the analysis of any broker or bank. To fail to do so is almost certainly to be assured of being part of the market herd—part of the 95 percent of share-market participants who either barely break even or lose.

A lot of time has been spent on this subject; however, this is probably the most significant factor in the success of a warrior trader. The way of the warrior trader is demanding, and it requires the ability to think independently about the state of an economy and seek out real-world economists and analysts. Finding these allies is invaluable in attaining a real understanding of the fundamental forces driving any market.

# CHAPTER 2

# WARRIOR TECHNICAL ANALYSIS

## TECHNICAL ANALYSIS IS STILL AN ART

Technical analysis looks at the technicals of a share, currency, or market—that is, the charting patterns and technical indicators made up from movements in the actual price of that market—to form an opinion about historical and future price trends. The movements of forces about the battlefield are subject to certain technical limitations, just as they have always been. Battle is a timeless art and one that has always been governed by technique. Fortunately, on the battlefield of financial markets there is a precise art that is an invaluable framework for understanding how fast forces can shift and to what extent their power has been expended or reestablished.

Even the best-laid plans for battle, which have incorporated a superior understanding of the majority of forces arrayed, can go awry if some basic principles and understanding of some of the forces at work within the battle have been excluded. One can enter the fight and experience totally unexpected twists and turns—it is important to always remember that the enemy possesses the ability to surprise. For the warrior, it is often the case that the battle may turn, quickly going in the direction opposite to that expected. It takes experience and some expertise in technical analysis to be able to gauge whether a counterattack by the enemy, be they bulls or bears, is a fade, a bluff, or something more sinister and potentially damaging. The true warrior trader is able to triumph through the application of both the warrior spirit, in accord with knowledge of battlefield tactics, and strategy.

Technical analysis is so often lauded as the "science" of financial markets—so much so that many treat technical analysis as a type of mathematical solution by which share markets and other markets can be deciphered. Not surprisingly, then, many who endorse this analysis will strive endlessly to perfect their trading model. However, this is exactly the same error that pervades the thinking of most market economists—who believe that if they can apply theoretical models more skillfully than others have done, unlimited success and triumph will be their reward. In both cases, generalizations based on past experience and backward-looking data are applied to the current situation. By definition, data used by economists are backward looking, and so too is the price action already established on any chart being read by a deluded technical analyst.

Technical analysts, who so often see themselves as rising above the earthbound thinking of economists, are actually perpetuating exactly the same errors. Both are seeking to make a science of what is an art. The processes of markets, like the processes of society, are so complex and, more important, are evolving so quickly that it is not plausible that a single theory or model could keep pace or accurately predict the future, except on very rare occasions. I argue this despite knowing that there are some technical models that can make prodigious forecasts. But this fact creates a kind of myopia, making us feel as though we have finally discovered that magical key to untold wealth. In reality, what we have discovered is that general theories can sometimes work almost perfectly.

## The Art of Using Technical Models

If we look at the price charts of any market and begin to search for examples of the technical analysis theories you have no doubt learned and studied in books and articles and the odd seminar, it is easy to start getting quite excited. Examples do abound. Now for the reality check, however. What we have just done is, with a particular image in mind, search for this image in the charts of markets that cover enormous sample periods. As we do this, we also *want* to find such images. Our study is, without question, subjectively and even emotionally biased.

Given the vast array of markets and now prodigious price history available to anyone who cares to look, it is not at all surprising that someone teaching Elliott wave theory, for instance, can show you spectacular examples of how perfectly the theory has worked on a variety of occasions. It is difficult not to become excited. Here is someone saying that markets follow these patterns, and—Hey! Presto! Look at this!—it works. The problem is that one could probably get a monkey or a dolphin to generate a curve shape of some form. We could then look for that same shape in terms of historical price action and—guess what?—there would be real-world, accurate examples of our monkey's or our dolphin's market curve.

But this does not mean that technical analysis does not work. On the contrary, I find technical analysis extremely useful. It is important to remember that technical analysis, like economic fundamental analysis, is an art, and an evolving one at that.

*It is important to remember that technical analysis, like economic fundamental analysis, is an art, and an evolving one at that.*

It is important to remember that technical analysis, like economic fundamental analysis, is an art, and an evolving one at that. Static mathematical models that have had great success in the past rarely, if ever, make money in the future. Many a black-box model is sold to investors with claims of tremendous profits over the last one to two years. Yet these same products invariably do not make the purchaser of the model a profit over the following one to two years. There are two reasons for this.

First, if I sit down at a computer for 20 minutes, I will probably be able to generate two or three new models that had fabulous returns over the last 18 months in some market. It really isn't hard. Finding models that will make money over the next 18 months in those same markets, however, is a lot harder. I am not sure such models exist, and if they do, they are so difficult to find that anyone who does so is highly unlikely to sell them. The harsh reality is that a model that has generated significant profits over the previous 18 months has a very high probability of generating losses over the forthcoming18 months.

Second, warrior traders know that great success can come only as the result of sincerity and the constant application of a winning trading approach. In fact, warrior traders happily accept individual battle losses, and even occasional strings of losses, as they know that they have developed their trading approach over many years during the cut and thrust of actual battle. Having experienced success using their own approach in the past, warrior traders trust that this success will come again. It is this ingrained knowledge and experience that allows warrior traders to develop a belief structure that is not easily shaken. When the occasional string of losses is experienced, there are usually an abundance of reasons—perhaps, for example, the losses are due purely to the laws of probability and the imperfect and fluid nature of the economic environment. But warrior traders do not focus on defeat—they are steadfast and relentless. This courage and persistence places warriors in the right place at the right time to maximize the profit opportunity presented when their winning approach swings back to work effectively in a particular battle. The victory is inevitable, and it is as much the result of a psychological attitude as it is of material tools.

It is for this reason that the purchaser of a trading model stands little—I suspect, zero—probability of success. Even if it were a winning model that could guarantee a long-term winning formula, at the experience of the first string of losses, the purchasers would probably find themselves floundering psychologically and emotionally, wavering to the point where the loss of confidence finally causes them to stop using the model—and probably just when the model was about to have a win. This means that the chances of the model succeeding are reduced by the traders' lack of dedication.

This is perfectly normal human behavior. None of us is happy to carry out an activity that is not of ourselves. The more we are the creator and controller of whatever activity we are involved in, the greater our degree of engagement and commitment.

"So," you might be asking, "what does all this have to do with technical analysis?" I'm coming to that. But first, it is important to note that the errors that bring down so many traders can be recognized, and that a greater and deeper understanding of the processes involved in markets can be established, meaning that the path to warrior trader status and subsequent wealth can be clearly defined. Both fundamental analysis and technical analysis make a contribution. Neither is the complete solution.

Entering the world of technical analysis with this knowledge means that we can see a truth that can add tremendously to our trading success. So, unlike many a textbook on technical analysis, this chapter will devote itself to a few simple methods that I have found to work in the long run. Of course, they need to be applied with the mind and attitude of a warrior—that is, the subject must be treated as an art.

## CLASSICAL THEORY TECHNICAL ANALYSIS

The underlying assumptions of technical analysis are as follows:

1. Given similar circumstances and conditions, people tend to react in a similar manner.
2. All fundamental information is available to, and absorbed by, market participants rapidly. That is, all the fundamental

views, real or not, are already in the price. This leaves only emotion as the unknown and influential force.

What many technical analysts do not fully appreciate, or appreciate at all, is that it is the difference between reality and consensus fundamentals that gives major market movements their power. The emotional swings that are so often given status by technical analysts actually occur only around what is a fundamental price shift or trend. It is this fundamental force constantly in the background, and usually very consistent in power, that is at the heart of any trend. However, despite failing to recognize the significance of the real fundamentals, technical analysis provides the clearest measure of immediate emotional bias and has been shown to deliver excellent overall forecasting performance.

My own view of technical analysis and markets in general is slightly different from textbook theories. I believe all the various theories are essentially describing similar phenomena. Whatever school or schools of thought analysts or traders choose to follow should ultimately be dependent on what appeals to them and what they are comfortable in understanding completely. All market theories have significant overlap—most are simply describing the same phenomena using different language.

## Using Classical Technical Analysis

Rather than concentrating on individual technical methodologies, warrior traders see through the array of technical theories to a deeper truth. As I will describe here, there are processes that give rise to repetitive patterns of behavior in our markets. Warrior traders do not deviate into a particular obsession with one particular discipline of technical analysis but instead see all the theories as potentially having some value. Ultimately, warrior traders know they must choose the theory that works best for them. We are all individuals, meaning that the different languages and approaches to the market will have varying degrees of attractiveness to each of us. Finding the one, two, or even three approaches that we feel some affinity for and can quickly incorporate into our developing personal battle style is of vital importance. Contrary to common belief, applying a greater number of approaches or technical tools into one trading approach can be detrimental. It is better to thoroughly understand and be familiar with one to three approaches. In this way you develop a warrior-like sense of how the market is looking on the basis of your preferred methods. This gives the warrior an advantage over the trader who mechanically applies a vast array of technical tools.

*Warrior traders do not deviate into a particular obsession with one particular discipline of technical analysis but instead see all the theories as potentially having some value.*

On the battlefield, there is no time for hesitation. Hesitation can mean defeat. It must all flow as one—action and reaction must become an organic and synchronous exercise. Our fundamental understanding, our technical analysis weapons, and our conclusive instinct must unite in a timeless and artful fashion to deliver winning blows in a steady stream of success.

What the various theories of technical analysis have in common, and what is essential to successful battle, is the belief that there are repetitive patterns of behavior in the price action of markets. This can be seen after even a cursory glance at market charts. However, every market is different, and every trend within each market is different. While the textbook application of these theories will provide only limited success, the real-world battlefield application of some theories can signal the end to the enemy. Warrior traders identify the pattern of *now*—that is, the pattern of this particular market and the battle at this particular time.

When developing an understanding of immediate price action, it is essential to remember that all markets develop rhythm. When that rhythm alters, it usually signals a significant change in trend. Identification of that rhythm—that is, the current pattern of behavior—can be aided by the broad and flexible application of some technical analysis theories. But, ultimately, understanding of a market's rhythm is an art—an art that anyone can develop but few have bothered to. It is just one of the arts learned by the warrior trader. However, on the day of the battle and in the midst of furious action, it can be the most important skill of all.

## THE THEORY OF TECHNICAL ANALYSIS VERSUS THE REALITY

Technical analysis is the study of the price action of a market. It is an art of observation from which a great many useful things can be derived. In order to determine a market's overall direction, and the potential extent of future movements in price, past behavior of the price action of that market can be an insightful guide—although, as already discussed, it is important to remember that the sum of information taken from technical analysis can only be historical and is not predictive by nature. To the warrior trader, this knowledge of the dual reality of markets—that is, the history-future that is unfolding in real time—is an invaluable and essential element in winning the trading battles and thus the profit war.

The study of technical analysis works, then, to fine-tune the warrior's instincts with regard to the next movement of the market; however, this form of study also highlights the distinctions between the different disciplines of battle and the varying weapons required. Technical analysis helps warrior traders decide on their methodology, their specific art form, and the weapon of choice for them as individuals. I will discuss the specialization process warrior traders must proceed through a little later, but for now let's look at what really does work on the battlefield of markets as far as technical analysis is concerned.

To my mind, technical analysis has a significant and marked advantage over fundamental analysis when it comes to practical trading in financial markets. Technical analysis does, however, perfectly coexist with, and is complementary to, fundamental economic analysis. Observing an animal in its natural habitat is a useful way of developing an ability to forecast its future behavior. Saying this, some may wish to study the same animal through scientific dissection and the endless analysis of the individual organs of that creature. But it seems somewhat obvious that the former approach—that of studying the animal in its natural environment—will be far superior to the art of dissection in terms of predicting the animal's actual behavior in that very same habitat. In some ways, I believe the dissection that invariably forms part of any fundamental analysis draws us away from the objective at hand—that is, to understand and predict correctly the behavior of the animal itself. No matter how correct our fundamental insights are, we must get the price movement right in order to achieve a material, rather than a purely intellectual, reward. Both art forms have their place. For the moment, however, the important point to digest is that the observation of market behavior through technical analysis in the real world can be valuable in predicting where those very markets will go in the future.

*No matter how correct our fundamental insights are, we must get the price movement right in order to achieve a material, rather than a purely intellectual, reward.*

As self-evident as this may seem, there are many who ridicule technical analysis—especially those who occupy the halls of economic academia and the research houses of most major banks and financial institutions. Personally, I find the situation bewildering. It has always been a puzzle to me why so many economists have trouble accepting the value of technical analysis—it is not a threat, but a concurrent resource.

## The Warrior Trader's Trend Secret

Technical analysis, as I use it, is the only way of successfully monitoring and managing the emotional ebbs and flows around what I call the *fundamental shift rate* (FSR). The FSR is simply the overall pace of adjustment, or price angle, of a major trend. Thus, the FSR, expressed as an angle to the horizontal, tells traders the direction and strength of the current price movement. The FSR is the midpoint of the channel defined by the high- and low-point extensions of the trend. Looking at Figure 2.1, you can see what I mean by the FSR.

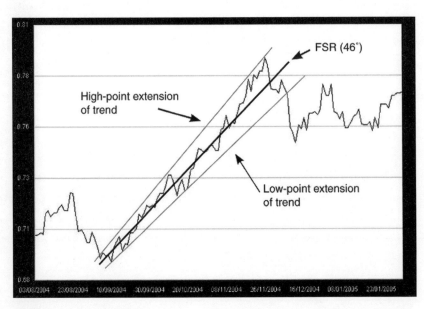

**FIGURE 2.1**  Fundamental Shift Rate—US$/A$ (*Source: www.ozforex.com.au*, copyright OzForex Pty Ltd. Reproduction with permission.)

The warrior trader's secret when it comes to technical analysis is in being able to understand exactly why there are such enormous swings and such volatility around the central FSR of a market or around the overall trend. This secret held by the warrior trader also explains why the extreme points of these swings can end up producing two parallel trend lines. In fact, the FSR is the midpoint between these two trend lines.

Interestingly, the parallel nature of the extremities of market trends has been one of the daunting challenges confronting mathematicians who have tried to suggest that financial markets are random in nature. The existence of parallel price point behavior creates a powerful mathematical argument that price action is not random. In observing price action, it is undeniable that these extremities, or *tipping points*, appear regularly—either repeatedly as points of support and resistance or in the creation of discernible channels of trending price movement. (Points of support and resistance are discussed in more detail later in this chapter.) Such observations would lead me to contend every day of the week that financial markets are not random. Warrior traders also know this and have a keen understanding of the forces that produce a trend and what some call volatility but what warrior traders call opportunity.

## Anatomy of a Trend

For a moment, let's have a look at the macroelements that are usually at play in trending markets. Inevitably, this is a journey into the pop psychology of a trend and the market crowd that participates in it. What is most relevant, though, is that warrior traders know and understand each element of the trend prior to its unfolding and are able to position themselves time and time again to achieve maximum profit from the movement. Many will profit at different times in small and even largish amounts, but only the warrior will systematically take money out of the market on each turn of events.

### Unexpected Fundamental Pressure

When a price trend starts, it is usually already running late relative to the fundamentals—in all probability it will be lagging behind the fundamental economic reality. Rather than preempting the future, markets are usually preoccupied with simply trying to figure the future out, and often in a quite emotional way. At the start of a new trend—for example, a bull trend—it is usually the case that the fundamental forces have already shifted in real time, but the market has been busy overshooting the previous bearish reality. But once the market crowd recognizes the new dominant fundamental forces, it has to do two things: first, get out of the now-unjustifiable short (that is, sold) positions it is holding because of its previous bearish beliefs, and second, actually buy so as to get long and try to take advantage of the bull swell in the offing.

### True Believers Reassert

Once everyone who believes in the new paradigm takes a position, there will appear to be a pause in the trend before it proceeds. Now, remembering these are early days in a new trend and many participants will see this upward movement as a bounce in a bear trend rather than a fresh bull trend, those who are bearish may misread the price hesitation and decide to sell again. This will, naturally, lead to a down move. This movement can be severe, and price can often go all the way back to near the starting point (the absolute low) that had preceded the start of the new bull trend.

### Everyone on Board

The new fundamental paradigm is in full swing, however, and the same forces that were pushing the market higher due to the imbalance in supply and demand again begin to dominate. As the market moves higher this time, the psychological impact is magnified and becomes much more powerful. The buyers are greatly encouraged as the previous low holds and begins to look like a handy support point (and a double bottom for any revisionist technical analysts out there), and the bears are discouraged at the failure of the market to break to new lows as they had expected. Now we have a market that is psychologically or emotionally leaning to the upside, overlaying a bullish fundamental reality. The converging of these two currents (fundamentals and emotions) can create the most powerful move to the upside of the whole trend, but there is a lot more still to come. As this very fast uptrend continues, more and more participants have greater confidence in it. Even fringe-dwelling market observers, such as everyday mom-and-pop investors, may eventually be drawn into the excitement.

### Exhaustion Consolidation

At some point, however, it is inevitable that, despite the immense size and nature of modern financial markets, the finite number of participants who can sustain the buying pressure will simply run out. This leads to an exhaustion phase. This phase is when basically everyone who could possibly want to buy into this stock or market has already done so. There is simply no one left to buy. In such circumstances, it does not matter whether any fresh news is bullish or not, as there simply is no one left to buy. The market, unable to sustain itself, now begins to fall back on any selling that occurs as a normal part of the market, with sellers looking to recoup funds for all manner of reasons.

As the market approaches this exhaustion point, it simultaneously reaches the maximum potential energy to the downside. The potential energy to the downside is a direct consequence of all the buying that has been done—some for real business purposes, but the most significant portion for speculative purposes based on the bullish emotions that were flowing at the time and the perception that this would materialize as capital appreciation.

Speculation is, of course, successful only when unrealized profits are made concrete through the closure, or the sale, of those positions. Thus, the more buying that has been done into a market, the greater the potential energy to the downside should there be fresh bearish news or should simple market exhaustion occur. Added to this is the potential for significant selling pressures as speculators race to realize profits.

It is worth noting here that the underlying fundamental forces to the upside have not altered one iota during this period; however, the market continues to move as a result of the emotional energy that flows from the interaction of people who sustain it. All that has happened is that, first, market participants have recognized the new bullish paradigm and got more and more wound up about it as the market continued to move higher. After the exhaustion, however, a high degree of confusion usually emerges. For the latest arrivals, there will be losses on bought positions. There might even be some short sellers who begin to make small profits again. It is this state of discord that results in what is usually the most drawn out, and quite choppy, price action of the whole trend.

### Final Overshoot

The bull trend has not yet concluded, however. The underling bullish fundamental forces are constantly, gradually, readjusting the balance, recovering the balance, and then relentlessly shifting the net pressure again to the upside. Once again, the nonbelievers convert and the market participants begin to buy aggressively. They have made money before from being long and so are now quick to get on board again. Typically, this movement results in the last sharp overshoot to the upside.

The market continues to gather momentum to the upside until ultimate exhaustion is in place and/or the fundamental forces have again returned to the downside. Indeed, it is sometimes the case that the overshooting nature of the market to the upside can swing the underlying fundamental forces to the downside. This is because the market can also be shown to have a cause relation to the fundamentals of which it is often the effect. At this point the whole process may begin again to the downside as a major bear trend. Alternatively, it could simply be a period of hesitation on a grander scale, of a greater quantum, to that which followed the penultimate exhaustion high.

## The Five-Wave Structure of a Trend

As the preceding analysis shows, a trend consists of a five-wave structure. In an uptrend, for example, the first wave is the result of unexpected positive fundamental pressure. The second, corrective, wave occurs as the true believers of the previous trend attempt to reassert themselves. The third, and most powerful, wave occurs as the market at large recognizes the new bullish fundamental paradigm and rapidly tries to jump on board. The fourth wave, which follows the inevitable exhaustion of the third wave, occurs perhaps for no other reason than because of the dearth of financial participants. The fifth wave occurs because the underlying fundamental pressure has not subsided—although its enthusiasm in overshooting the mark can create pressure on the fundamental forces to such an extent that the fundamental pressure can itself be reversed.

Here is a summary of this series of five waves:

1. Unexpected fundamental pressure—impulsive
2. True believers reassert—corrective
3. Everyone on board—impulsive
4. Exhaustion consolidation—corrective
5. Final overshoot—impulsive

To some readers, the parallels of my trend analysis to the tenets of Elliott wave theory will be obvious; however, I would contend that warrior traders have a deeper knowledge of the process that allows them to maximize the opportunities presented by these swings about the underlying fundamental shift rate. This trending process is also not something that occurs in isolated instances; rather, it can be seen repeatedly, from within the grand scale of many years to within the minutiae of just a few hours. While the pattern does not replicate perfectly, it is there like an evolving musical pattern left only to the skillful trader to play it by ear. The warrior trader, understanding the process and not just the simple technical wave count, can adjust in real time to where the market is at, and therefore remain ahead of the enemy in every stage of the battle.

*The warrior trader, understanding the process and not just the simple technical wave count, can adjust in real time to where the market is at, and therefore remain ahead of the enemy in every stage of the battle.*

The two human emotions that dominate in this trend, and any other market trend for that matter, are fear and greed (discussed in Chapter 3). But it is not simply a case, as many writers and so-called experts suggest, of people being greedy then fearful in rotation. Rather, it is a far more complex interplay among the recent experience of the market, fundamental forces, market positioning, and then fear and greed that dictates the price action. Ultimately, while fundamental forces will always drive the market in the long run and will always win out, the swings and roundabouts are driven by an overlay of other forces. The good news is that the whole process can be understood. It is also worth remembering that the markets are never irrational—they just sometimes appear to be as they try to catch up to what is really happening.

## Impulsive versus Corrective Waves

The distinction between *impulsive* and *corrective* waves is paramount to the reading of any chart in technical analysis. An impulse wave is identified by its clear directional movement, covering a lot of ground in a relatively short period of time. Any hesitation during an impulse wave is relatively brief, and the market rarely dips back during these periods of hesitation once a new high or low has been made. Corrective periods, by contrast, are easily recognized by their quite whippy and chaotic price action. If there is any period in markets that tends toward the random walk that some theorists have suggested—that is, that markets are completely random in behavior and without rationale—it is during these corrective consolidation phases. Indeed, while various theories are promulgated to explain what is happening during these corrective periods in price action, I have yet to find one that is able to predict the internal price action of these phases in real time. There are, however, several that, in hindsight, can be applied in a relatively successful manner.

In general, impulse waves are the domain of the trend traders, and corrective periods the domain of range traders. We will discuss this important distinction—which will greatly impact the profitability of your personal trading—in detail a little later.

In summary, you should note that markets follow an endless cycle of underestimating the fundamental forces in the direction of the trend and then systematically overpricing those forces. Swinging from one extreme to the other, our actions compounded by the conflicting emotions of fear and greed, we view price action as a constant intertwining path of emotion and reality. In simple terms, the market gets ahead of the fundamental forces at work, starts to doubt itself, and promptly turns in the opposite direction. The market eventually hits the wall that is the still-trending fundamental force, begins to believe again and reinvests, only to finally fall victim to the changing underlying fundamentals. This is the process that causes significant alternating swings around the central fundamental shift rate.

## PRINCIPLES OF TECHNICAL ANALYSIS FOR WARRIOR TRADERS

Some of the general principles of technical analysis that I have found over the duration of my trading career to be reasonably reliable are discussed in the following section. It should be remembered, though, that the immediacy of price action is such that stagnant rules and artificial constructions built to support predictive theories are always incomplete.

### Continuation Patterns

*Most corrective or consolidation periods are what can be termed* continuation patterns, *rather than* reversal patterns.

If price action moves up from a lower level before entering a prolonged consolidation period, the market is likely to again move up to fresh higher levels after this period. My experience suggests that the continuation of the trend in the same direction is true by a probability of 59 percent, and this view is supported to some extent by Elliott wave theory. The reverse is true for bear markets. This may not seem like a major advantage, but indeed it is. Some of the world's most successful warrior traders may have only a 59 percent battle success rating, meaning that only 59 percent of their trades are winners. However, one thing that average market participants never quite seem to understand is that it does not matter what a trader's win/loss ratio is— all that matters is the size of the winnings in comparison to the losses. Warrior traders can indeed exist on a win/loss rating of only 59 percent, principally because they ensure that the size of their average win is several times the size of their average loss.

This is one of the deftest skills of the warrior trader. True warrior traders are able to exit a difficult battle with minimal injury, and when dominating a battle, they do so absolutely. A mixture of occasional minor wounds and more common total victories will see gains compounded and lead to an enviable mountain of profit and immense wealth.

> *True warrior traders are able to exit a difficult battle with minimal injury, and when dominating a battle, they do so absolutely.*

## Support and Resistance

*Areas that were once support/resistance become resistance/support when broken.*

An area of support is simply a price area from which the market bounces upward, perhaps once or several times. On occasion, this price area may be quite precise and be at a certain absolute level; however, more often it will exist as an area that is the width of a few points or cents. Further, once a support area is broken (that is, the market falls to a lower level, as the support could no longer hold the selling pressure), the price area will commonly become what can then be classified as an area of resistance to the upside of price action. Somewhat like a mirror image of support, resistance is an area that a falling market has difficulty penetrating. Once price action breaks through a support barrier, when the market tries to rally and move back above the old support level, it will invariably encounter a level of resistance at the point of the previous support level. Selling interest at this level serves to contain the buying pressure and results in the market falling once more.

The same process, in reverse, can repeat itself—whereby a resistance level can become support.

To warrior traders, this seemingly simple principle can be quite valuable. The warrior trader recognizes that if the bullish movement on the battlefield is maintained, the battle will continue to take fresh ground rather than move back into the previous area of heavy fighting. In other words, once enemy lines have been breached, those lines should now hold as one's own if the direction of the battle is maintained.

Should the taking of enemy lines not hold, warriors recognize that the forces arrayed against them may be greater than first calculated. In this instance, warriors may decide to withdraw altogether from the battle that is producing unexpected loss of ground rather than risk suffering significant losses through continuing to fight.

## Current Pattern of Behavior

*All markets settle into repetitive patterns of behavior. But it is the current pattern of behavior, rather than any textbook theory or label, that is relevant and useful.*

We have already discussed this point, but it needs to be emphasized. The identification and recognition of the current pattern of behavior are the ultimate objective of value-adding technical analysis. Instead of ascribing a textbook formula, which can only ever be a mere generalization, warrior traders avidly seek to understand a market's—a battle's—particular individual pattern of behavior in the current moment. In doing so, they seek to grasp the emotional state of the market and so gain a significant advantage. The opportunity for true insight into the likely future course of a market is to be found in the current pattern of behavior, or in the recognition of this market's rhythm in this moment.

## Break in Rhythm

*Settled patterns of price behavior collapse only when a new trend is starting. This can often be caused by a fundamental shock or can sometimes precede awareness of the underlying fundamental shifts.*

The major strength of technical analysis is not so much its forecasting ability, which is sometimes remarkable, but its disciplined way of alerting the analyst to an "incorrect" market view. Technical analysis allows warriors to protect themselves. Like armor, it is not perfect; however, choosing to enter the battle without it is a decision fraught with danger. A strategy based purely on fundamental analysis can be an arduous trial, as a falling market without any fresh news or data provides no delineating point at which fundamental analysts and traders can justifiably exit their view. As the market moves lower, it simply appears cheaper to buy. For a technical analyst, a break in rhythm or a break of a previously identified support level would signal that the market was moving to a new range and was not near the bottom of its potential at all. While the price may seem low relative to recent experience, it is actually high relative to the likely new, lower, range—meaning it should be a sell.

From my point of view, all major trends are fundamental price shifts evolving within a broad band of price action, the details of which, and submovements thereof, can only be understood effectively using technical analysis.

Markets are made up of people, which results in emotional patterns of behavior being played out every day in the course of market interaction. These emotional patterns overlay, and sometimes disguise, the true fundamental price shift or trend direction. Technical analysis is an art that has real-time practical value in assessing market conditions. It allows warrior traders to be specific in their points and styles of attack, and to know precisely on which occasions it may be best to retreat for the day.

Technical analysis is a major discipline of study for warrior traders, one that allows them to live to fight another day.

# CHAPTER 3

# EMOTIONAL PRICE ACTION

As Chapter 2 showed, technical analysis is useful for assessing current market conditions, where emotions can cause the true fundamentals to be hidden. Price action is certainly emotional. It is about markets in motion, which easily flows into a clever combination of the new *e*-economy and *motion* to arrive at *e-motion*. The more sound argument is, of course, that markets are made up of people, and people arguably are emotional rather than logical creatures—whether we like it or not. When applied to a large gathering of people—for example, a market crowd—the argument for emotion over logic becomes all the stronger.

Therefore, price action is ultimately driven by emotion—both the emotion of the herd and that of the individual. Although, as I've suggested previously, economic realities are the underlying forces that determine the value of markets in the long run and, for the most part, generate long-term fundamental price shifts, that long run is usually too long for most traders, whose pockets are not deep enough to allow them to wear the aberrations that are part of any major price shift. The shorter the investment time horizon, the more significant the role of emotion in determining the market price action.

## THE MARKET IS ALWAYS WRONG

Many have argued that the market is always wrong. Indeed, the market must by definition always be wrong because its participants are emotional, rather than logical, creatures. A natural conclusion emerges: The market can never rest at its objective, logical level. As emotional beings, we are perhaps incapable of determining such an objective, logical level anyway, even if we delude ourselves to the contrary.

When the market does rest, it is at an emotionally comfortable level and is therefore inherently unstable. I would argue that only a person with a highly trained mind who has spent many years studying meditation techniques could maintain a reasonable mood consistently for any period of time. A market made up of thousands of participants has no chance.

Price action is, to use a cliche, the bottom line. It does not matter one iota if you manage to get the economics right while the market goes in the opposite direction. This difference between what the market "should" do and what it does do is seen all the time. Why? Simply because of the age-old laws of supply and demand—the actual gross buying versus the actual gross selling in the market—as opposed to theories on the potential movement in the broad economy. (I have used the term *gross* because in this age of huge individual-entity market participants, it is sometimes the case that, although there are more buyers than sellers, the market goes down because the sellers' positions were bigger.)

> *It does not matter one iota if you manage to get the economics right while the market goes in the opposite direction.*

The economics of a country are but one influence on a market—regardless of whether we are looking at equities, bonds, or currency markets. Other factors that come into play are the market's performance relative to other economies and markets and even the global political environment. Where all these factors lead, however, is to one elegant place: the mind of the market participant. The final computation of all these factors is then filtered through the enigma of that human condition, emotion.

The way market participants use emotion to filter information varies from day to day, depending on all sorts of factors—from the weather to whatever market position is already in place. Participants who are long a market will largely filter out any bearish news developments. Against this, participants who are short a market will focus almost completely on bearish news. Yet all information is absorbed. The net combined effect of all the fundamental forces and all the emotional filters is the collective view of a market—that is, its current price. Is it any wonder that prices are almost always unstable? This innate instability of markets is, in effect, the "emotion" of the marketplace.

Perhaps a slightly more contentious point that I would also offer for consideration is the differing emotional structures pre-existing in different markets. As traders, we are increasingly trading globally. A phenomenon I have observed among market participants is actually nationality based and even relates to some sectors of the markets' political beliefs as well. It is not uncommon, for instance, for traders in the United Kingdom to be slightly more negative in their attitude toward their own economy and the release of data on their economy than perhaps U.S. traders would be about similar data outcomes regarding the U.S. economy. There seems to be a natural pessimism about U.K. trading behavior, compared to a slight state of enthusiasm in U.S. trading. It has been observed that, generally speaking, different cultures have varying psychological profiles. In these two examples, neither is realistic, but both present opportunity. If we understand that U.K. trading will tend to overreact to negative data and perhaps slightly depreciate positive data, then we can look to take advantage of the temporary price overshoots thereby created. This principle works similarly, and in reverse, in the U.S. markets.

Financial markets are very much a product of laissez-faire economic thought. It is only natural that any sample of market traders would then tend to discover that on the political spectrum the bell curve is skewed slightly to the right. This explains, in addition to the more obvious point, why markets tend to dislike left-leaning governments around the world and embrace governments that are more conservative. Again, this creates opportunity. As a warrior trader, you must always be independent in thought when approaching the market. Observing a market overreact to good news in a conservative government economic environment relative to the treatment of good economic data in a less than conservative environment can be a factor in increasing short- to medium-term trading success. It is all emotional, even on levels people are not always aware of.

How can you monitor and keep up with this combined unstable emotional force? You cannot gauge a market precisely; however, you can get an effective handle on its current direction and whether it is bullish or bearish. The tool for achieving some awareness of the overall emotion of a market is technical analysis. The other reasonably effective method I am aware of for achieving this is to simply watch trading screens for a few hours after a piece of economic data has been released. This allows you to see whether the market has moved in the direction suggested by the data or not, and to what degree. (I suggest a few hours because immediate volatility after an economic release can be like fool's gold, and it is a lure that can entice many.) A short-term trading strategy can be centered around the price at which the market sat just prior to the data release. If the market moves in response to the data, and the price movement is valid, then it should not retrace beyond that immediately prior to the release price level. If it does, then there is probably an even bigger trading opportunity in the direction opposite that which the data release indicated.

## GREED AND FEAR

I've touched on the emotions of greed and fear already, but these twins of the market need to also be covered in any discussion of emotional price action. Without doubt, greed and fear are the two most extreme emotions experienced in a market; however, almost every human emotion is discernible and present in every market on a daily basis. What affects the market is the degree to which each emotion is present and the fluctuations in these levels. While a market can be said to be responding based on greed or fear on a particular day, the use of such terms by some market commentators to describe specific and significant market movements can be quite misleading.

Often a bull market is described as a "market of greed," but the reverse may also be true. In today's heavily fund-driven equity markets, a fresh range break to the upside may see strong follow-through buying that is actually being driven by fear. If fund managers have been in a market that, until now, believed that some fundamental indicator such as earnings multiples were too high, they may suddenly experience the fear of having missed the boat as the market heads north. They will definitely experience the fear of underperforming their competitors. Thus, a bull market can be primarily fear driven and a bear market greed driven (as sellers rush to lock in the highest possible profits). It all depends on the consensus expectations that existed before the fresh range break or new trend development.

Indeed, if you extend the argument, it becomes quite plausible to suggest that almost all major market moves are fear driven. When the market crowd gets a market right, the resulting fresh price movement created by the confirmation of the consensus view is usually quite limited. On the other hand, the price action that results when it is suddenly realized that the crowd's consensus expectations were badly misplaced can be sustained and even excessive. The driving emotional force behind these larger movements is fear.

## EMOTIONS AND THE USE OF FUNDAMENTAL VERSUS TECHNICAL ANALYSIS

As discussed, technical analysis is the pure study of the price action itself, and as such, its use is more appropriate when traders are looking to comprehend the emotional swings and roundabouts that all the fundamental forces contribute to but, in anything other than the medium to long term, rarely dominate. While the fundamentals are real and remain the underlying driving force, in the context of daily, weekly, monthly, and even quarterly profit reporting, only technical analysis gives you not only a handle on the forces at work in real time but also a reminder of the truly dominant fundamental force. The term *dominant* fundamental force is used because this captures what is the greatest weakness of fundamental analysis and the greatest strength of technical analysis. At every point in time, as discussed already, there are both bullish and bearish fundamental arguments and forces at work. As there are no clearly assigned weights to any particular variable, which is the more powerful is extraordinarily difficult to quantify on paper.

The only way to deduce the dominant fundamental bias in real time is to study the price action using technical analysis—in particular, the big-picture view provided by a long-term chart of the market's price action. By *long term,* I mean a chart showing the price action for at least the previous 10 years. While five-year charts down to hourly charts all have their place, an awareness of the long-term levels is essential even for the day trader.

From looking at the long-term charts, the dominant fundamental shifts should become self-apparent. What should be particularly clear is the extent of the volatility—that is, the swings and roundabouts around the underlying trends. Again, this is where technical analysis comes to the fore. It can allow you to monitor and understand—and even sometimes foresee—the extent of a correction or fresh trend.

In effect, while fundamentals drive markets, technical analysis allows us to trade in markets. The fundamentals of the modern world are simply too vast, too complex, and too rapidly changing for anyone to be able to understand it all in real time. Further, it is this real-time understanding that is essential in both successful forecasting and trading.

*In effect, while fundamentals drive markets, technical analysis allows us to trade in markets.*

There is a further analytical skill that comes only with a long period of experience: intuition. There is no doubt that those who can intuitively read the market are the true warriors. The scope of this book, however, is to help with the development of skills that will, with time, lead to the experience and refinement of that elusive quality of intuition.

Markets, at least in the short term, are operating largely out of emotion, which is the domain of technical analysis and which is also the time horizon in which most traders are interested.

# CHAPTER 4

# QUANTUM VIEW

This view of markets is entirely of my own making, and although some may find it perhaps a little abstract, I think this is a perspective that can provide a constant underlying basis to one's overall trading approach. The individuals to whom this approach appeals will find it invaluable.

While not a field of study that can be easily applied to trading in financial markets all the time, the discipline of quantum physics does have a contribution to make that can prove insightful. Further, being aware of this alternative and additional view of markets can add a greater depth and color to other disciplines such as fundamental and technical analysis. Warrior traders do perceive markets with a holistic sensitivity that would leave many other traders scratching their heads. And while this may not be for everyone, there is a simplicity in the quantum physics approach that seems to resolve many of the complexities of market price action.

Through looking at markets using a quantum physics approach, it is possible to discern an even deeper underlying structure on which market behavior operates. Indeed, viewing markets from an energy and information perspective is a direct lift from quantum physics. This kind of approach also reflects aspects of Eastern philosophy.

## INFORMATION AND ENERGY

The information and energy theory of market behavior argues that information has an impact on market behavior. No surprises so far. But it also argues that the market energy levels have an impact on the future behavior of the market equal to those of information already received and future information that becomes available.

> *. . . market energy levels have an impact on the future behavior of the market equal to those of information already received and future information that becomes available.*

In other words, if the market has a low energy level, even dramatic fresh information entering the market will have a limited impact on prices. Conversely, when the market is in a high-energy state, even relatively insignificant fresh information can trigger a large move, which in turn can lead to a rolling snowball effect. For example, as more and more participants reach their thresholds of pain at which they must act—that is, close or reverse their positions, often simply because other participants have had to do so at an earlier price level—the market gathers momentum. At these times, the market snowballs of its own accord.

By *fresh* information, I primarily mean political or economic comments by leading figures or the published findings of reputable statistical publications that are out of line with market expectations. In this context, statistical results in line with market expectations are not fresh information. In the case of an extremely high-energy market, however, mere confirmation of an expected outcome could be enough to trigger a significant price move.

### Determining the Energy Level of the Market

The next question is obvious: What determines the energy level of a market? A market can certainly be said to be in a state of high

# PART II

# WARRIOR WISDOM

energy after a long period of consolidation. Recalling an earlier analogy, the dam is full because water, or energy, usage has been low. While brief consolidation periods replenish energy to some degree, the creation of a high-energy state requires a significant and sustained period of consolidation. Once this high-energy state has been achieved, given an appropriate catalyst the market can move into a sustained trend in either direction.

A long period of consolidation suggests that all market participants are happy to continue to trade at current levels. Neither buyers nor bears are dominating or stressed. If the market begins to break the range one way or the other, a snowballing trend can develop. Such a market is primed to respond to any fresh information, be it bullish or bearish.

Another form of the high-energy state, but one that can move in only one direction, occurs toward the end of a sustained trending period. Some markets simply reverse because there are so few players left to add weight to the direction of the trend. At this point, there is a very high potential state of energy in the direction opposite to the trend—that is, a high potential for reversal.

For instance, within any sustained bear trend, there will be holders of short positions who at some point need to close out their positions. There are also usually a great number of buyers who have been sidelined as they wait for some sign of the tide turning. The market can be said to be in a potentially high-energy state to the upside, as any fresh information that is bearish will have little to no effect, while any fresh information that is bullish will see an exaggerated and instant market response.

## WARRIOR TRADING AND INFORMATION AND ENERGY THEORY

In light of the preceding, it is possible to successfully approach the market from the standpoint of answering these two simple questions: What is the energy state of the market? And knowing this, what is the potential impact of fresh information on price action? Using this approach, market action will provide clues as to whether the market's energy state is high, medium, or low, and what the likely impact of fresh news would be. Recent fresh information will also provide clues, if one examines the level of importance and relative impact of such news.

We have all heard the stories and seen instances in the market of bullish economic figures being followed by a bear market. The usual response from market commentators is that the market had already "priced in" the figures and so did not need to respond. However, according to the approach suggested here, the phenomenon would be described as an energy-exhausted market to the upside. This means that the energy level for a bull move was nonexistent, but the energy level was at its maximum potential for a down move. Hence, even fresh bullish news could not carry the market any higher. When trying to understand the energy level of a market, simply examining the price action following fresh news provides major clues for the short- and medium-term outlooks.

In summary, the information and energy approach best describes the underlying structure upon which all market behavior operates. Markets appear sometimes chaotic, sometimes orderly; sometimes they appear in line with the textbook theories, but more often not. Underlying this, markets have discernible patterns of behavior that can be understood through analyzing the impact of information and understanding the current energy in the market. This is because the effect of fresh information will always depend on the energy state existing at the time of the information's arrival.

# CHAPTER 5

# THE TRUTH OF MARKET SUCCESS

**S**peculation is a noble pursuit.

Sometimes, in the rush to participate and the attempt to make our fortune, we fail to consider just what markets are. Even if we do have some knowledge of what this game of trading in markets is really all about, it is well worth taking the time to remember the core function of stock markets the world over. The first purpose of markets is not, as many suppose, to make us all rich! Markets were first created to provide a way for people who need to buy or sell a commodity, or to raise or invest funds, to do so—and this remains, at heart, their primary purpose.

Speculation by traders comes after this essential need; however, this is not to say that it is a parasitic pursuit. Speculation does indeed add a magnificent aspect to the functionality of markets. This great addition is that speculation makes markets efficient and liquid. Thus, attempting to profit from mere price movement in a market—that is, speculating or trading—is a noble pursuit and one that is necessary for the health of markets.

The pursuit of long-term trading for profit, often more broadly referred to as *investment*, has been a major driver in the creation of the high levels of liquidity that exist in markets today. This increased liquidity makes the flow of capital, via bond, equity, and currency markets, to productive purposes more efficient. Because of this, speculation—or, to use the term with more positive connotations, investment—has reduced the cost of doing business, and has thereby encouraged and assisted the expansion of the global economy.

**71**

## THE CHOSEN FEW

Noble though speculation may be, it is certainly a path to which many are called but few are chosen. This aspect of markets—harsh to the many, but extremely beneficial to the few—emerges purely because most participants are not market-savvy. Most traders simply operate as part of the herd and have no personal awareness or self-identity as such. As aggressive or as antagonistic as this may sound, it is nevertheless the reality, and acceptance of this is necessary to eventually graduate to warrior trader status.

*Most traders simply operate as part of the herd and have no personal awareness or self-identity as such.*

Naturally, though, it is a truth that is often unrecognized by those to whom it applies. Members of the herd do not see themselves that way because if they did, they would doubtless change their behavior immediately. As previously discussed, the length of any trend in any market can be extended precisely by the actions of the crowd—or may even exist purely because of these actions.

It is sometimes said that everyone gets what he or she wants from the market. Whether they are consciously aware of it or not, some simply wish to be seen as trying, struggling, and even failing in the markets. Some seem to want huge wins that enable them to celebrate wildly, followed by equally severe losses that enable them to enjoy the sympathy of loved ones and/or colleagues. Some want to achieve small wins and persist for years with the eventual result of breaking even. Some want just that one big win so they can then go and do something else. What all of these participants have in common is that, even if they are not decapitated in the first few conflicts, they will never achieve great share-market success. Still others want to test their wits, their all, on one of the last relatively pure and level battlefields in contemporary business.

Emerging from this last group will be the victorious few, those who have relentlessly applied their knowledge in the pursuit of victory and have risen to the top of the pile as if standing on the corpses of their fallen enemies. These are the warrior traders.

## Proportion of Market Winners

It is difficult to know the actual proportion of market participants who win over the long term. My own estimate, and those of several well-regarded traders and warriors, puts the figure at about 5 percent. That is, just 5 percent of market participants consistently win over the long term, year after year. This figure sounds devastatingly low until one recognizes that it is because it is such a low figure that it must indeed be correct. How else would it be possible for the few, the warrior traders, to build the enormous fortunes that inspire all of us to compete for the prize? A success rate of 5 percent suggests that 100 percent of the money invested by all market traders will end up in the pockets of just the top 5 percent. In reality, it is probably more like 85 percent of the wealth in the market goes to the top 5 percent, as there are no doubt some traders who continue to break even. Nevertheless, when one considers the degree of success and wealth some traders are known to have accumulated, it becomes clear that this rate of 5 percent is most probably correct.

Look around you. Of your colleagues and friends who you know trade in markets, it is likely that only 1 in 20 will be a long-term winner. Only 1 in 20 will consistently win on an annual basis, and do so over many years to come.

Even before you consider the question of whether you are that 1, let's consider the other 19. The real breakdown is obviously unknown; however, it is possible to make general predictions. Of the 19, usually 3—that is, 15 percent—will break even over the long run. The remaining 16—or 80 percent—will lose consistently. Some will lose everything they have. Many will lose such a significant sum that it will have a serious impact on their personal lives. This is no lighthearted matter or subject. Of the 5 percent of participants who win, many will go on to exert economic, and perhaps political, influence over their communities as a result of their tremendous victories.

This fundamental urge to compete, and to claim the rewards once victorious, has existed for as long as humans have existed. It is a primal willingness and eagerness to prove oneself upon the battlefield, and to reap fortune and power as a result.

## STAND OUT FROM THE CROWD

This is the core of markets, and there is no point in trying to suggest some intellectual motivation. Any such intellectual competitiveness is launched from a more deeply seated motivation that has more to do with the desire to remove yourself from the masses and stand out from the crowd. This primal urge is also why trading can become wholly absorbing.

This also helps to explain why the characteristics of the ageless warrior can also be found in today's seemingly sophisticated and highly intellectual market winners. Warrior trading means accepting that market trading is a battlefield that should be approached in the same way as a real warrior would approach a real battle. Many traders will converge on the battlefield. All will have weapons (of varying effectiveness), and many will be fluent in their technique. However, few will fully focus their minds so that they are always ready to strike or evade in order to be truly victorious.

When it comes down to the mind being the only differentiating factor, it becomes plain why psychological theorists suggest that all those involved in markets successfully get what they really want. Some may want pain and get it; a few want financial success and get it. More and more, what the vast majority appear to really desire is simply to be able to have conversation that will impress their colleagues, relatives, and friends. To be seen to be a player would seem to be all that most people really want. This explains why the vast majority do not accumulate vast fortunes, and why the herd will make or lose money relatively comfortably. Consider what it is you really want from markets—comfort in the herd or the acquiring, through concerted exertion, of warrior trader status.

# CHAPTER 6

# WALL STREET MEDIA NEXUS

## CONSENSUS EXPECTATIONS

When it comes to expectations about markets, there is no doubt about who is creating the consensus. Most market participants are completely unaware of the process that leads to them being told by their broker or the media that the "market expects" or the "consensus expectation" for a particular market or economic data release is such-and-such. Indeed, warrior traders do not really want all the market participants to know this process because if they did, very few would take any notice of the predictions. If this happened, a major factor in the creation of the immense opportunities offered by markets to warrior traders would be removed.

The story of market consensus starts with each of the major global investment banks. While you may think your bank or broker provides you with a unique view on markets—and all of them claim to—this is not usually the case. It is truly amazing how many large national banks and brokerages take their research and market view leads straight from the global investment houses. The pressure to conform comes with the clamor of global media corporations and their willingness to report the failure or success of available research (the earlier discussion of fear as a major motivating factor can also be applied here). The biggest reason for this lack of originality, however, is that such organizations do not spend as much on their research teams as the global investment banks do, and other research

79

teams simply cannot compete with the depth of research done on every aspect of every market by the global houses and the detail provided from this. Most of the rest of the global research community simply spend their time sifting through the global investment bank research, of which they are subscribers, to discern the key points and thereby market themselves to their clients as "clever and informed" market economists. This is why you can hear exactly the same mantra repeated by a series of market economists from different organizations across the media on any given day.

## The Development of the Consensus View

But this is a digression. Let's return to the beginning of the consensus view within each particular global investment bank. Where does the bank forecast come from? Almost without exception, the bank view comes from a rather large committee of specialists who are experts on the full spectrum of factors that affect markets—from South American interest rates to inflation expectations in Poland and back to the Dow Jones in New York. It is largely the same process in each of the major investment banks in the United States, Germany, France, and the United Kingdom. While there are some large investment banks located in other centers such as Tokyo, it is really just a small number of people from these four nations who drive the consensus expectation in virtually every market in the world.

Having been part of this process, I have no doubt that few others taking part in it have read the works of John Maynard Keynes, despite the occasional reference to his work that appears in the research provided. It was Keynes who cautioned that trading by committee was a sure path to failure. The justifiably well-respected team of which I had the honor of being a member at a global bank consisted of 27 market economists and strategists. This number was actually relatively low in comparison to some of our competitors in this select group, who had much larger teams than ours and sometimes significantly more resources. Nonetheless, this group of 27 would meet once a quarter to decide on and produce the bank's forecast for the next 12 months or longer for all aspects of global financial markets.

Basically, all the participants were locked in a room for two solid, grueling days, where the level of contribution and debate ranged from the inspired to simply regurgitating yesterday's newspaper. Eventually, and often wearily, the consensus of the 27 would be found, formed from the full spectrum of views on a particular market and from bullish and bearish predictions. In the end, the team of 27 would unanimously applaud the agreed-upon specific forecast.

Even from a distance, it is obvious that this painful process is fraught with the risk of error. Even before it begins, the process may be fundamentally flawed. There is the risk that a sample of 27 market observers from around the world might simply reflect what the broad market is already thinking. It is almost impossible for the participants themselves to offer an objective analysis, as they have usually been a part of the market and were absorbing the market consensus prior to the two-day meeting. In other words, it is impossible for the opinions of the attendees to be anything but subjective to the prevailing culture.

In light of these fundamental flaws, let's now look at the next stages of the process. Toward the end of the forecasting debate, there would be a last-minute consideration of what key competitors were known to be forecasting. This was not necessarily because the view of any competitor was considered to be of value—as their equals, we knew better than that—but because we knew that if anyone was going to get good press and media exposure, it was likely to be the investment bank that offered a forecast that was the most different from or more extreme than all the others. To some degree, there was a self-reinforcing feedback process occurring between the global investment banks and the forecasts they offered vis-a-vis their competitors in the forecast tables.

As if that is not bad enough, there are politics in markets as well. Relationships with major clients and central banks, and even with major political parties around the world, can influence the forecasts of investment banks. Some investment banks are large donors to certain political parties. While there may not be explicit instruction, the chief economists of any of these firms are likely to be aware of such donations and are therefore unlikely in research to talk about the likely market impact should that side of politics suffer defeat. Research propounding the benefits of the victory of that political group may even surface.

## The Distribution of the Consensus View

Once the forecasts were established, they would be released to clients and the media. Market participants would then begin to receive research from their local banks or brokers and/or regional or national banks or brokers. All the research would include similar information about an economy and what this meant for particular markets. At the same time, the same views would be aggressively promulgated in the media. With such consistent bombardment from all angles, is it any wonder that market participants become quite convinced, even passionate, about a certain possibility in the market? It starts to seem as if the market in question would be incapable of doing anything but what the brokers and media are saying it will do.

## TAKING A CONTRARIAN VIEW

This avalanche of consensus affects even other, smaller invest-ment banks. A certain view can very quickly become so well known and widely disseminated that anything expressed in contradiction to it is almost seen as heresy—or at least a sign that the person expressing the contrary view does not really understand markets. As someone who strives to offer an objective view on a market, I frequently offer a viewpoint contrary to that of market consensus—which can make people who have spent the last month being bombarded with one particular view feel quite bewildered. There is a saying that a lie told often enough will be accepted as the truth. In the markets, a view repeated often enough can be accepted as a sure thing.

> *There is a saying that a lie told often enough will be accepted as the truth. In the markets, a view repeated often enough can be accepted as a sure thing.*

## A Contrarian Position on the Australian Dollar

When the Australian dollar collapsed in the late 1990s, I was perhaps the most aggressive forecaster of its decline. The Australian dollar had been trading at 80¢ and looked to be on its way to 82¢ and then 85¢—and, indeed, this was my initial forecast. Then I realized that the true fundamentals, as opposed to the consensus fundamentals, painted an entirely different picture. Because of continuing high trade and current account deficits and the significant moderation in interest rate levels, it was highly likely the Australian dollar was about to move into a major long-term price decline. Generally, high interest rates relative to other countries lead to an inflow of (albeit short-term) overseas investment. This offsets the trade deficit and produces an appreciating currency—even while the otherwise fundamental vulnerability of the currency due to the worsening trade performance continues to grow. Once interest rates moderate, the currency is left highly exposed. This process is frequently repeated in currency markets and has been one of the main drivers in the fall of the once mighty U.S. dollar in recent years.

Back in the late 1990s, while I did not immediately change my forecast for the Australian dollar, I did send out an advance warning to clients that there was an alternative perspective to the still-favored bullish outlook. By studying long-term price behavior and patterns, I thought that should the Australian dollar move below 78¢, it could signal that it was about to collapse. When the dollar fell, against consensus expectations, through 78¢ I already knew what this could mean and how far the currency could decline. At this point I began to practically scream from the rooftops that the Australian dollar was on its way to 68¢ or even 65¢. This was considered a wild call, and even clients who usually followed my advice to the letter began to doubt my ability. As the dollar tumbled lower—to a lack of reaction, or stunned inaction, from most market participants—it became obvious that my first forecasts were actually too conservative. The dollar would be going even lower. I was the first to predict a level of below 60¢ for the Australian dollar, and then to finally forecast a 48¢ low with risk to 45¢. While the 45¢ prediction got more publicity, the central target of 48¢ turned out to be quite accurate.

When I first started predicting that the Australian dollar would fall to 60¢ and eventually the 48¢ low, my forecasts were front-page news, especially in the business sections of major Australian papers. Yet the view was so contrarian that the managing director of the international investment bank I then worked for sat on my desk with a copy of the newspaper in which my predictions were quoted and simply said, "You had better be right." It is not easy to go against the headwinds of consensus; however, it is often the most lucrative tack, as it suggests everyone else is the other way and will have to turn if they are wrong.

*It is not easy to go against the headwinds of consensus; however, it is often the most lucrative tack.*

## A Contrarian Position on the Euro

When the euro was first formed out of the constituent currencies of Europe, it was truly remarkable just how one-eyed and confident market consensus was that it would be strong. I traveled through Europe visiting clients in the months before its float. So intense was the view from absolutely everyone I met with that the euro would go up once it had floated that only one conclusion could be reached. It was clear to me that the euro would fall dramatically in its first 12 months. In this case, it was the consensus view that totally determined my market view, due to the sheer intensity and confidence of the market. When everyone is that confident of their beliefs and talking so openly about them, you can be sure of one thing: They have already bought. If everyone has already bought (sorry to put it so bluntly), how can it go any higher? In effect, everyone had already bought euros by buying the deutsche mark and French franc, the most liquid currencies that would be automatically converted to euros on the first day of the new currency. Some of these buyers would become sellers to square their positions, and then there were the real sellers—the importers and people investing overseas from Europe. What were they doing? Waiting for the euro to rally so they could sell at a better level.

My forecast was for the euro to rally for one to three days and then collapse for the next 12 months, predominantly because all the buying for the next 12 months that European exporters would normally do had been done in advance and because currency traders had also already bought into the euro. Such was the conviction of the consensus view. Again, forecasting the way I had meant that it was a challenging time for me. This time, working for a European investment bank, I was warned that my forecast could cost me my job. Fortunately for me but not for the bank—which was positioned, like everyone else, long the euro—the currency did go up for three days and then collapsed for the following 12 months.

## WARRIOR TRADING AND CONSENSUS FORCES

Fundamental forces drive markets; however, when consensus has a high level of conviction, it is this that may drive the market in the short to medium term, regardless of the long-term fundamental reality.

As discussed, consensus comes from a handful of global organizations through the internal process of committee compromise. Even though right from the start the quality of such forecasts is highly doubtful, with no one else to quote, the media quickly swamps the globe with these views. The process then feeds on itself, as a particular view is quickly accepted by the vast majority of investment houses and is therefore entrenched in research everywhere.

Warrior traders love the opportunities presented by consensus forecasting. Although it may initially appear to be a self-fulfilling prophecy, the more entrenched and excited a particular consensus view, the greater the opportunity of a windfall profit when eventually and inevitably the market breaks from it.

# CHAPTER 7

# THE POWER OF MARKET POSITIONING

As well as the fundamental and emotional forces, another difficult-to-quantify factor that becomes more important the shorter the time horizon of your trading is market positioning. By market positioning, I mean the net long or short positions held by traders in a market. In some markets, these data are readily available; however, in others, the data are something traders must estimate for themselves.

## THE SHORT-TERM VALUE OF DATA

Global financial markets are huge and the participants varied. Gaining a handle on how a market is positioned can be extraordinarily difficult. As discussed earlier, often the best guide is the market itself and how price responds to releases of fundamental data. If a market fails to rally on the release of data that are better than expected, perhaps that market is already very long, and vice versa. Warrior traders must be conscious that all markets, by their very nature, are layered and that different types of participants can assume opposite positioning because of their different investment time frames.

Be warned, though—you need to watch a market reaction for a considerable time period. Any market will almost always run in the anticipated direction after an economic data release for the first 15 minutes to hour. It is only after the initial price adjustment that an insight into current market positioning can be gained. What the market has done by the close of trading of that day is usually the clearest guide.

## THE IMPORTANCE OF MARKET POSITIONING

Market positioning can become the most important determining factor in achieving trading success. As already discussed, in any market a continual run of positive fundamental news can end up producing a situation where absolutely everyone who wants to buy in that market has done so. In effect, there is no one left to buy. So when the next piece of news comes out—even if it is better than the market expected—no fresh buying can occur. There are, however, plenty of longs (that is, buyers) looking to take profit at some point. The longs then become, in fact, potential sellers or, in market parlance, shorts. This desire to consolidate profit can mean that the market will fall and even accelerate to the downside after more good news. This process is discussed in greater detail in the next section, and what will become obvious is that the way market participants are positioned is a factor not to be ignored. Although market positioning is perhaps more of an art than a science, it is an art well worth mastering.

## WHEN GOOD NEWS IS WIDELY EXPECTED, THE MARKET IS VULNERABLE TO A FALL

In any market, at any time, there are buyers and sellers. Some need to act at particular times regardless of events; however, most, such as business participants and speculative traders with varying time horizons, can wait for what they believe will be the best moment for them to buy or sell. If the media and market research papers are awash with expectations and forecasts that a

THE POWER OF MARKET POSITIONING

particular stock is going to have an excellent profit result, what are these business participants and traders most likely to do? The following sections look at the effects of the expectation and release of positive news, based on the market positioning of different market participants.

## The Buyers Looking for Stock

Clearly, those who need or want to buy will be fearful of not being able to buy at the current price levels. At the same time, these buyers will be excited by the riches they envisage they will make after they buy and the profit result comes out. This is a powerful combination of emotional forces. Fear is driving traders away from any notion of delay. Excitement and greed is propelling the trader to invest as much as possible. Traders are only aware of the perfect "logic" of their decision to buy. After all, the company is about to release a great profit result, meaning it's obviously a good decision to invest in this enterprise. The end result is that those who were considering buying do so quickly, and frequently in greater volume than they had originally planned or need to.

## The Sellers Holding Stock

On the other side of the fence sit the sellers for business and speculation. How does their world look? Unlike the buyers, the sellers believe they have it made. They are under no time pressures, as they believe the expectation that the market will rally handsomely after the profit result comes in to be perfectly logical. They plan to just wait to see how high the market goes before taking any action, and they are starting to think they will make even more money than they had originally calculated.

Straightforward logic dictates that, for the duration of the period that starts when the market first hears that a good profit result is likely, buyers in the particular stock are going to be aggressive and most sellers passive. The market price will tend to rise in this environment, and to all participants the price action merely confirms their expectations, so the belief in their perfect logic intensifies. The process of buyers being aggressive and sellers passive gains even greater momentum and becomes self-reinforcing.

## The Profit Result

By the time the result actually comes out, everyone who has wanted to buy this stock, and even those who were planning to buy after the profit release, has already done so. At this point, every single buyer would claim it would be foolish not to already be in the market. At the same time, absolutely every market participant who wants or needs to sell but can delay doing so has delayed. This leads to the situation where, in a complete reversal of common market belief, on the morning the profit release is due there are only waiting sellers in the market. The buyers have already dealt their hand.

Assuming the good news does unfold, what happens next is that everyone—the longs and sellers both—watch their screens in barely contained excitement. Both are expecting to do extremely well. Everything is going according to plan. Often, they watch for a while and nothing happens. There may be a small price rise but usually not a lot of volume in actual trading. They all continue to watch.

Who do you think is going to act first? The sellers, of course, because they have yet to do what they have or want to do for business or speculation. Now here is the key twist—the sellers are, in fact, everyone. The buyers have become sellers, almost without noticing, and there remain only sellers in the entire market. Of course, many of the buyers are there for the long haul, or so they suppose. Still, there are several buyers who were looking to make a quick buck in the hours or days after the profit result was released. Now, after some time has passed, these longs begin to wonder if perhaps that old adage "Buy the rumor, sell the fact" is perhaps what they should be doing.

At this point, those who need to sell begin to execute their orders. Next in line, the short-term speculative longs start to follow suit. The stock collapses as more and more people try to lock in the highest profit possible. Business reports on the evening news are aghast at the carnage and at the fact that investors who at the outset had been so obviously right end up losing money in a bizarre market movement.

## The Warrior Trader

Throughout this whole process, warrior traders have been active. In most cases, warrior traders would have bought even before the market began discussing the potential of a good profit result for this stock. If not, warrior traders were probably the first to buy, doing so swiftly as a reflex rather than after extended consideration and through being able to foresee a familiar scenario.

Being aware of how the market is likely to position itself is how warrior traders profit. As warrior traders understand the process laid out here, they will take profits a day or two before the result is actually released. This allows them to sell into the last of the buyers while there is still reasonable liquidity. Remember: Warrior traders usually have large volumes of stock to trade as a result of having already made significant fortunes, meaning that they require a significant amount of liquidity to enter and exit the market. Still, for warrior traders it is an easy play. The herd did what it always does, as it never seems to learn. The warrior trader grows richer, and therefore stronger, yet again.

## Better-Than-Expected News

The preceding scenario was based on the result being positive, as the market expected. It is, of course, possible that the result was even better than expected—would this not have led to a profit for the buyers after all? The short answer is no. The reality has not changed—if everyone who wants to buy into a market has already done so, it does not matter how good the news is, there is no one left to buy. There are still only sellers. The best that could occur in such circumstances is that the existing bid and offer orders may be raised. There may even be some excited longs who do even more buying. But the euphoria is nevertheless short-lived. Everyone who wants to buy has done so. Everyone who wants to sell has yet to do so. The market subsequently begins to drop away.

> . . . if everyone who wants to buy into a market has already done so, it does not matter how good the news is, there is no one left to buy.

## The Big Move

Now for the double whammy! What if the news is less positive than expected or, worse than that, even negative? This is when the real fun for warrior traders begins. Warrior traders would have been sitting in readiness, having already anticipated such a possibility. When the news is flashed on the screens, the fingers of warrior traders have hit "sell" even before the warrior traders themselves have consciously processed the news. In fact, true warrior traders often find themselves having to check again what the actual result was after they have already sold.

There is no way the members of the herd can keep pace with this speed. The herd is in a state of shock—both longs and new would-be sellers. Openmouthed, the herd watches as the price drops away from them. They wait for a bounce, but as soon as there is one, someone else (no doubt, a warrior trader) has beat them to it again and sold before they could. The market falls again.

## End Result

The end of this story is predictable. Warrior traders absorb the last of the herd's selling as they buy back their shorts.

The medium-term outcome could even be that the market goes on over time to make fresh highs as a more normal balance is returned to it. Yet many of the herd—who were long on the fundamental expectations and then forced out near the bottom of that sharp and nasty correction—will simply be watching from the sidelines, unwilling to be burned again as they mutter bitterly that they were right all along and that it was just a silly market. These same people are not long the stock now due to their negative experience. The fear of a repeat experience has kept them away from this particular stock.

This is another difference between the behavior of warrior traders and that of the herd. While on many occasions warrior traders experience losses, they never allow such experiences to psychologically debilitate them or keep them out of winning trades in the future.

# CHAPTER 8

# CONSENSUS CONCENTRATION, BELIEF, AND REALITY

## SURVEYING CONSENSUS

Another insight into market positioning and the value of determining the consensus view can be gained from the activity surrounding economic data releases—but this time from the activity in advance of the release. Surveys are readily available from media services that quantify the expected responses to the release of each specific data item. While the consensus number is valuable in determining the net view of the overall market, it is also worth looking a little deeper. If you examine the details, these surveys usually show how many forecasters are bullish and how many are bearish. They also show whether there is a wide divergence in expectations or relative agreement among participants. If the forecasts are grouped tightly together, it suggests that the market has a high degree of confidence.

From a trading perspective, this means that an unexpected outcome should have a major impact on the price of the underlying currency or stock, or on the market as a whole. If a significant majority of forecasts are bullish, for example, a bullish outcome is likely to have less market impact than a bearish result. It is the nature of the economic release relative to the consensus expectation, combined with the price action after the release, that provides the best available guide to overall market positioning in a particular stock or currency. Once the process of market positioning is understood, this knowledge can be used by warrior traders to profit in similar situations in the future.

## Concentration within Consensus

Knowing how to read and act based on the degree of concentration within consensus is the mastering of this art. The consensus forecast for any economic data release is just a number, and this will be adopted as the overall market consensus. While it looks the same for every release, there are secrets within. There are often quite significant differences (and distinctions) in the detail behind various consensus forecasts. I call this the *degree of concentration* within the consensus. Regardless of whether there is a wide range of forecasts that are evenly distributed or a narrow concentration of forecasts from all contributors, an overall final average and consensus will be distilled by the market. Unless the detail of the survey that led to the final consensus number is looked at, traders have no way of knowing whether the market is diverse in expectation or highly concentrated. This is important in understanding the potential price reaction to the data when they are released. When the actual result diverges from the consensus expectation, market price reaction will be dramatically different depending on whether the consensus expectation was backed by a concentrated narrow range of forecasts or by a widely dispersed one.

If the market is positioned over a wide range, unless the result is completely outside the entire range (which does happen), the whole market is not required to move toward what is an unexpected reality. If, however, the entire market was narrowly focused on a particular outcome and the actual result was different even to a relatively small degree, the entire market has to adjust to the unexpected reality. Obviously, the power of the movement will be significantly greater when the consensus is concentrated.

## CONSENSUS AND THE LEVEL OF BELIEF

While most of the market may be bullish in view and forecasts, it can be the case that few actually have positions set in support of this view. In such circumstances, the market maintains the ability to move quickly to the upside because, despite the bullish forecasts, the market is still short. This can happen, for example, when the expectations for a stock are quite positive but the stock will soon go ex dividend. This approaching event can be enough for potential buyers to hold off, waiting to buy at a lower level after the dividend. That may sound contradictory, but market price movements around dividends are not always what the textbooks suggest.

> *While most of the market may be bullish in view and forecasts, it can be the case that few actually have positions set in support of this view.*

Another example might arise if everyone is forecasting a currency to be strong because of its trade balance and the amount of investment flowing in but is concerned the country's central bank may intervene to prevent the appreciation of the currency. Again, the market might be offering bullish forecasts, but few, if any, participants are actually long. In the end, this is the potential buying power that may well see the central bank overwhelmed. Hence, the market can move sharply higher despite consensus being bullish if this consensus has not been acted on.

Consensus expectations are the bread and butter of warrior traders; however, what really distinguishes warrior traders in this area is their ability to discern the quality of the consensus view in terms of concentration and belief.

## CONSENSUS VERSUS FUNDAMENTAL REALITY

Hence, getting markets right is about finding the difference between the current (and likely future) fundamental economic situation and the broad market perception—that is, the consensus—of what that reality may be. Is there a variance between the reality and the perception of a particular market? If so, at some point the market will have to play catch-up, and that period of adjustment is likely to provide enormous profit opportunity for the speculator aware of this early in the game.

Sometimes the reality and the consensus perception of a particular fundamental backdrop are aligned. More often than not, however, they are either at odds or at least in some kind of divergence. It is then only a matter of time before they are forced to converge, and in most circumstances, due to the energy of the catch-up phase, the market is prone to dramatically overshooting the mark. This is the basis of all large and sharp adjustments seen in markets.

The interesting thing is that when the consensus is the same as the fundamental reality, there is generally not a lot of money to be made—the reality has already been accurately priced into the market. It is when the consensus differs from reality that significant opportunity presents itself. However, how is it that, given the high degree of communication in modern society and the advanced analysis of economies and markets, the consensus is frequently, let's face it, wrong? Understanding why the consensus frequently fails frees warrior traders from its often powerful influence, allowing a more pure and objective focus on major opportunities as they are presented as a result of this very failing.

**PART III**

# WARRIOR IN BATTLE

# CHAPTER 9

# WARRIOR MIND

The following section provides a summary of the main points already made throughout the book that traders need to remember in order to maintain the level of mental awareness and strength required to attain warrior status. Following this, we will look at specific factors the warrior mind must possess. Once the warrior mind is strong, warriors can move on to choosing their weapons, battle tactics, and total victory.

## THE WARRIOR'S SECRET

We already know that the select few, the warrior traders, behave differently from the herd and are able to scoop the herd's wealth. The first step in this equation is that the warrior trader gets the market right more often than the herd. Why is that? What does the warrior trader know that the herd does not?

In a word, *everything*. This is the case because the whole basis of the herd's understanding of the fundamental outlook relating to a particular market is often invalid. If we accept this premise, some interesting corollaries follow.

This dictates that the success pattern of broad fundamental views will tend toward random. For anyone who has been involved in markets for any length of time, this point should ring a bell. Economists as a group struggle to outperform a randomly generated selection of market outcomes. There have even been studies showing that a monkey throwing darts at a board can outperform economic predictions supplied by so-called experts. It gets even worse, however.

Because economic consensus expectations are a *consensus* (read "compromise"), those economists at the outskirts of the range are inevitably the most ignored. Yet it is sometimes in the fundamental analysis from these sources in particular that real gold can be found.

## The Warrior's Economic Secret

*The more you follow the consensus predictions, the less successful you will be.*

First, warrior traders understand the flaws contained within contemporary economic thought and how it is practiced with regard to markets. Second, warrior traders understand that even if the consensus expectation is on occasion correct, that expectation is already priced into the market by the herd. Therefore, even when the consensus expectation is confirmed by the economic data or the company profit result, there can be very little price movement in the direction of the expected result. The herd has already bought and is positioned long in the market ahead of the expected good results and can therefore only wait to sell at an expected profit after the event. The question they fail to consider is, where will the new buying come from? Usually it simply does not occur, and the herd finds itself fundamentally correct but watching profits quickly erode as the market goes down rather than up.

The herd then has to respond to the emotion of stress. The herd sells and sells, chasing a market lower even though positive economic confirmation relating to the stock, commodity, bond, or currency has just been released. Why does the price move lower? The answer is ridiculously obvious, yet how often do we see news reporters expressing surprise at such market price action?

## The Foundation of the Warrior's Economic Secret

We are here to make money by contributing to the efficient functioning of markets through our participation as speculators. The most effective way to make big money quickly is to separate yourself from the herd—to stand back and watch over the terrain with a warrior's gaze as the battle of buyers and sellers unfolds. The warrior, ever ready, will choose the best moment to engage in the battle, in a way that ensures victory even before participation has begun. This is the warrior's first great strength: the power of patience combined with the ability to choose his or her perfect moment. Later in the book I will discuss this moment of entry and how warriors come to decide on the weapon that is best for them. It is important, however, to be aware at this still early stage of this important first step. In effect, it puts the warrior's homework into perspective.

> *The most effective way to make big money quickly is to separate yourself from the herd . . .*

As we've seen, the purpose of the homework is to help the warrior get to know the terrain thoroughly. In markets, the terrain is the fundamental backdrop to the market under observation. The market is the war, and there are, of course, many battles fought on this terrain. These can vary from the long battles during the sustained trend or consolidation phase of a market to the shorter battle during a one-week trend and even some incredibly violent encounters that transpire within a single day.

The greatest strength warrior traders can have before entering the battle of their choosing is to know something the enemy does not. And as previously mentioned, there are two aspects relating to the fundamental reality of markets that are unknown by the herd. Warrior traders use both to their advantage. Warrior traders know that contemporary economic analysis of markets is successful only on a random basis, but can be useful in creating a countertrend trading opportunity when strong consensus expectations exist. The herd does not. Even though the herd frequently displays for economists and their off predictions a derision usually reserved for weather forecasters, the herd continues to worship at this same shrine. The shrine consists of a small number of economists from the major investment banks who promulgate their views. These views are then picked up by the other banks and financial institutions around the globe, with blatant plagiarism sometimes occurring. This pumping out of research to the global trading herd is also being picked up by the media, a powerful force on the human psyche, and is simultaneously regurgitated.

## The Power of the Media

Many studies have been done regarding the deep influence the media, and especially television, can and does have on people. To appear on television—as I am honored to do and, I must say, immensely enjoy—is to suddenly be taken seriously by a large number of market participants, who conclude, in effect, "He is on television, so he must know what he is talking about." In my case, I hope I do. The point remains, however, that the herd is constantly bombarded with research from a handful of economists, and then those very same views are reinforced via the media, particularly television. It is almost a brainwashing epidemic. Any army would do anything to get hold of a weapon that brainwashes the enemy into believing that if they go through a certain pass, they will be victorious. How easy would it then be to set a trap with deadly consequences?

Fortunately, warrior traders do not have to set the trap. The all-enveloping process of forming the consensus view is done for them. The spirit of warrior traders, however, is strong and is not easily influenced by such forces as mainstream economic comment and media regurgitation. Warrior traders can therefore wait and watch from on high, as the enemy files duly along the path below. The enemy, the herd, is mistakenly self-assured they are on a secure journey to greater riches.

Once a market—any market, on any scale—believes in a commonly held view, it is only a matter of time before the market breaks sharply against that view. The size of the move in the opposite direction is purely a function of the amount of disappointment in the forthcoming reality.

*Once a market— any market, on any scale—believes in a commonly held view, it is only a matter of time before the market breaks sharply against that view.*

In effect, the rewards to warrior traders for their patience are determined by the gap between what the consensus was expecting and what the reality turns out to be. And I am talking here about every scale of activity—from the futures pit in regard to a piece of data being released on the day to the global foreign exchange market expecting a certain economic trend to develop over several months, or even years, in a major economy. Warrior traders will reap the rewards at every level of every market.

The warrior trader can win in two ways. The first is simply by watching and waiting, as described, for the enemy to exhaust itself climbing a mountain pass to achieve a false dream and then attack as the enemy begins to turn back, already substantially weakened. Such is the way of the warrior opportunist.

The second, more difficult and often more rewarding, method is to actively and aggressively go in search of a correct contrarian scenario. If the fundamentalist warrior can successfully ascertain a different and significantly at-variance view of the future fundamental backdrop to a particular market, an immense fortune can be garnered quite rapidly. But don't be fooled; this is no easy task.

The most successful warrior trader of all seeks to combine the two approaches—layering patient opportunism on the back of a strong belief in an alternative fundamental reality. Remember the double-whammy scenario already mentioned? When great warriors perceive that the herd has it wrong and that the future will be quite different from consensus expectations, they will wait with maximum force readied for that moment when the herd displays the "stunned-mullet" price action behavior and begins to turn in disarray. While the herd is still confused and trying to come to grips with the hard evidence of a different fundamental reality, warrior traders have already acted in their own decisive way.

The resultant stampede in the opposite direction is a tremendous sight. The herd has to not only get out of the incorrect positions they so confidently first established, but also follow this up by attempting to regain the losses by going the other way. This usually results in a major fresh trend development that astounds commentators to such an extent that many a media story will be written about what is wrong with the market and what has caused it to act so seemingly illogically. I find it interesting that there are never any major articles about why the herd is wrong. The media propagates and is part of the herd, and self-criticism, though noble and a necessary part of learning lessons, is thought to be too expensive by those in the herd who make the errors.

We now move on to specific requirements of the warrior mind.

## YOUR MIND IS YOUR MOST POWERFUL WEAPON

Warriors stand still and effortlessly allow the chaos of the world to pass by. Warriors are prepared at all times to battle to the end, with all their wits, strength, and perhaps even luck. They enter the fray with a focus that inspires awe in their opponents, even as the warriors cut them down. But warriors do not celebrate their victories—they remain still and focused, ready to strike and enter a fresh battle, for they know that opportunity may arise at any moment.

> *Warriors stand still and effortlessly allow the chaos of the world to pass by.*

There is no doubt that a dog can be a fierce attacker and should be feared, largely because of its level of commitment. Once a dog begins to fight, it forgets all else and is relentless until victorious or defeated. In a similar but far more elegant way, the true warrior is also forgetful of self and fully committed to the immediate challenge.

Are you a warrior? Are you prepared to fully enter the fray, to battle endlessly until victorious, and then to battle again? This is what it takes to win in the market—tenacity, focus, and a stillness of mind that leaves competitors in awe.

## Using Your Tools

Tools of the trade such as fundamental economic analysis and technical analysis—and even for some still, inside information—are the modern market equivalents of the warrior's weapon, whether it be sword, bow, or hidden knife. On the battlefield, the other combatants, among whom are also some true warriors, lie in wait, armed with their own weapons. Your sword may be better than theirs. It may be made of the finest metal and crafted to a strength and sharpness that few have witnessed, yet the sword alone does not assure you victory. Your technique—that is, your technical analysis expertise—may be well advanced. You may have excellent execution through your broker and back-office procedures. You might think your logistical support places you in an invincible position. Still, you are not assured victory.

There is something else at play. There is something in the character of warriors that serves them through battle after battle. The warriors can be seen standing—perhaps exhausted, but still standing—upon the battlefield with many a slain enemy lying lifeless, or in agony, around them. Such a vision is most easily conveyed in modern financial market terms simply by looking into the futures pits. Literally, people have died on the battlefield that is the futures pit. (A minute's silence for a trader who has recently suffered a heart attack on the futures floor is a very real reminder of the battle.) On the trading floor of the world's futures exchanges, men and women triumph and fortunes are won and lost.

At the end of the trading day, it is easy for even a casual observer to distinguish the winners from the losers on a futures floor. It is also relatively easy for the trained eye to distinguish between the *true winners*—that is, those who win more days than they lose—and the other winners, for whom the day was a less frequent event than they would be willing to admit, perhaps even to themselves.

These other, less frequent, winners are the ones congratulating each other with broad smiles and boisterous displays. Their actions will consist of attention-getting large sweeps of the hands and the unavoidable backslapping. Their demeanor says "look at me." In contrast, the frequent winners—that is, those long-term successful traders who take money from the market on an almost daily basis, or the warrior traders—are identified by their more subdued and steadfast manner, in spite of which they stand out from the crowd. They are neither crestfallen nor verbose, but typically they are visibly afforded a degree of physical space that others are not. They are usually considering the consequences of their day's activities, and not just in terms of profit and loss calculations. The long-term winners will spend much time deep in thought about what they did, how they did it, and why. They will analyze both their perfect moves and their mistakes. They are absorbing the day's lessons so as to carry these lessons with them into the next fight, the next day of trading. They have been, and are constantly, involved in warrior trading.

## The Constancy of Battle

To practice the art of warrior trading, one must be a warrior at all times. To stop being a warrior, especially in the midst of a battle, is to be almost certainly slain. Such is the chaos, the constant confusion, and the involvement of all combatants that there is no moment to relax. Distraction is quite simply not an option.

This is no easy walk in the park. The level of commitment is not for the fainthearted. On the battlefield of trading, one can even lose one's life. This book is intended for those who truly want to participate in the most challenging activity that exists in the business world today, where judgment for your actions is immediate. In real war, as in sport, the result of your efforts is known extremely quickly, often in the blink of an eye. Your efforts may have been just a moment of engagement or an extended period of combat toward total victory, but the results are known immediately. The same is true of trading in markets, each and every day.

To trade in a market as a warrior, it is not enough to be clever about the fundamentals or technical aspects. Warriors need to think ahead about how others will respond to the same stimuli and where, therefore, the counterattack or dummy attack might come from. To win the war, warriors must enter into the minds of their enemies and develop a knowledge of what is going to happen. Many footballers will attest that they were in the right place at the right time to score spectacularly because they were able to see or sense in advance how the play would unfold. This is warrior thinking—or perhaps more accurately, warrior non-thinking. It is perfectly warrior-like to have a *feeling* about what is going to happen next. It is this awareness before the fact that can generate the seemingly instantaneous reaction of a great warrior to an event. The warrior mind has already decided what to do in just such a situation or development.

There is no denying, then, that warrior trading is the result of years of learning and practicing a particular form of combat—to the point where activity can enter the realm of nonthinking action. The constant application of this state of mind is what makes vast fortunes achievable in the markets. Few attain this level, but to move in this direction is a journey well worthwhile.

Conversely, to place all emphasis on the acquisition of knowledge and power—through fundamental or technical analysis, or other weapons—is to leave oneself exposed to the ongoing frustration of never quite making it. How many times have you heard people say that they had the right idea but missed the move or got stopped out? These are missed opportunities no trader can afford. To win over the long term requires warrior trading. It requires the letting go of learned skills in favor of the absorption of a holistic feeling for, and understanding of, the market.

## THE LOSS OF EGO

From Wall Street to local newspapers around the world, the financial talk is often all about the illogical nature of the market. Sometimes the feeders of the herd go even further and suggest that a particular market segment is responsible for the herd's having lost. Remember the 1987 stock market crash? The herd was decimated. And as is often the case when the pain is great, the herd searched for a scapegoat. In 1987 it was the program traders' fault. When the dot-com bubble burst, it was the fault of the dot-coms themselves—as if the world was suddenly surprised that those companies didn't actually make anything and that most of these firms had never been profitable, and as if the dot-coms had kept this a secret. The herd had known all along and even salivated at the sexiness of buying into purely virtual firms with huge overheads. Once again, the herd refused to blame itself for its losses and in so doing did not learn the valuable lessons being offered by the market.

Warriors, on the other hand, are always self-reflecting. They are always ready to take full personal responsibility for the results of their trading—to blame no other event or segment of the market and accept that the market is simply the market. Warriors' profit or loss is their domain, it is a result of their own behavior rather than the market. If warrior traders lose, they know it was because they were wrong. To begin to accept personal responsibility as a trader is to begin the journey to warrior trader status. What is remarkable is that very few traders can take this beautifully simple step. It means, of course, letting go of one's pride and relinquishing one's ego.

> *Warriors, on the other hand, are always self-reflecting. They are always ready to take full personal responsibility for the results of their trading . . .*

Interestingly, the loss of ego is the basis of all the great religions. It is also the fundamental principle that guides all great combatants and truly great warrior traders. While there have been some spectacular front-cover traders, the ones who amass fortunes year after year tend to stay in the background. At the very least, they display a simple and down-to-earth approach to markets if they are ever interviewed. Humility is essential for long-term trading success. Extravagant celebration and boastfulness quickly lead to one's wealth being returned to the market, as it is transferred to other, quieter and more focused, warrior traders.

This is the story, at least, of the warrior traders I know who are extremely successful. October 1987, for example, was my best trading month ever. Yet the proportion of trades I made that month that were correct is quite embarrassingly low. The great strength I have always had, however, is being able to let the winning trades run and ensure that they reach their ultimate potential. Saying this, in avoiding the emotion of greed, warrior traders are prepared to give up some of the last potential of a winning trade as a way of investing in the possibility of even further price extension and greater profits.

## ACCEPTING THE "HARSH" REALITY OF MARKETS

In October 1987 I was still reasonably young, and while I am not entirely proud to say it, to some extent I relished the massacre of the herd. It felt as if, as the herd had brought disaster upon itself, it was all in some way just.

This may sound harsh, but it is the reality of the market and, indeed, how warrior traders win. For several years one of the world's great warrior traders (though he would eschew the title) would ask me the same question, in exactly the same words, every time we spoke on the phone—which was sometimes daily. He would ask, "What do you think would hurt the market the most?" In other words, what price movement at that time would cause the most pain to market participants? To this day, he remains one of the world's great currency traders—he takes no prisoners and is a true warrior trader.

Is this harsh? No, not at all—and for some very obvious reasons. As speculative participants in any market, we are, essentially, looking to reap the wealth of our fellow participants. Markets are not a competition for which the prize is handed out from on high to the winner. The only prize that can be bestowed on winners is the wealth of their fellow traders. There is no point in maintaining any illusions on this subject. The warrior is always looking for the market's most vulnerable point. Knowing where the enemy's soft spot is—that is, the point where decisive and relatively quick and easy triumph would be ensured—is every general's dream.

## Why Enter This World?

It is also interesting to consider that it is this "harsh" reality that makes markets so attractive. Why is it that we are willing to enter into this chaotic fray of the many, on perhaps the most difficult battlefield of all, where all combatants are individuals? In some ways, markets are the ultimate evolution of the gladiator's pit. There is a very simple reason why we are willing to risk our wealth on this battlefield: Ironically, the reason is warrior traders themselves.

It is precisely because of the mere existence of warrior traders, and the media coverage of their enormous fortunes built through trading, that we are drawn to the market in the first place. We risk our wealth because we believe our intelligence and our wits will make us rich like the warrior traders we have heard about. Yet, as already discussed, it is a challenge to which many are called but few are chosen. The situation is analogous to swarms of moths being drawn off course by the bright lights of a major city. It is this very process of attraction that enables the huge piles of gold, which are amassed from the wealth of the herd, to be piled in just a few places, at the feet of the warrior traders. The warrior traders attract entrants into the game and then usually end up taking the small parcels of funds that these entrants contribute and adding them to their existing mountains of wealth.

The 1987 crash, like all others, was just and constituted an opportunity for the herd to stop, reassess, and learn. But, of course, the herd didn't do this. A decade later, the big lesson could have been learned via the bursting of the dot-com bubble. And the bubbles just keep coming—be they in oil, property, or currency markets. At the time of this writing, the value of the U.S. dollar has been falling for three years, a phenomenon that is itself the result of a classic bubble mentality. The same processes occur again and again. They are a function of human psychology and, as such, can be identified and anticipated.

## Institutional State of Mind

For those of you who work for, or are managers in, a large institution such as a bank or other trading house, these brief comments—though perhaps aggressive—should be of particular benefit. While the trader-to-manager communication process is not an easy one, if both parties can adopt a warrior philosophy— that is, one of brutal honesty where the focus is on what is called *the bottom line*—then untold riches can accrue to both.

Success at trading in markets holds a particular challenge for large institutions. Anyone who has been involved with a large trading-room environment knows only too well the mismatch of views and knowledge that often exists between senior manage-ment and traders "at the coalface." To be successful, warrior traders must always flow with the markets, constantly reacting as their instincts suggest. The highly educated but inexperienced eye—usually belonging to senior management—may view such a trader with a high degree of skepticism. The trader may well be interrogated about the thinking behind a particular trade— particularly, of course, if the trade was a losing one. The warrior trader—that 1 person in 20 who is capable of making money over the long term for the institution—may well find it difficult to respond satisfactorily to such questioning.

The senior manager, for example, may refer to news com-ments that were bullish a market and suggest, therefore, that the trader's short position in the same market was irresponsible and unintelligent and constitute evidence of an inability to fulfill his or her role in the institution. It will, of course, escape the senior manager's awareness that such bullish headlines are more com-monly associated with bearish price action, due to the complex interplay of market consensus expectations, the prepositioning, and the closing of positions, as we have discussed earlier. The trader might even be unaware that he or she had been sublimi-nally gathering such information and that this is what drove the instinct or gut feeling to sell. Hence, the trader may find it difficult to articulate the reasons behind the position.

As a result, the one true warrior trader in the trading room might feel harassed, losing the ability to maintain a constant state of focus and readiness and suffering the slings and arrows of many a competitor/enemy. In the end, the warrior trader may well be decapitated by the institution he or she has served.

The reverse situation can also arise, whereby poor traders can always justify their positions on the basis of seemingly sound economic argument. It is often the case that traders who compile histories of losses but also strong economic arguments are appreciated by senior management, since they tend to think alike. Less-accomplished traders may remain in place, treading water or losing, for many years. This is often the underlying cause when, on occasion, massive losses are "suddenly" discovered in a major trading room. Meanwhile, the warrior trader has left and found a more appropriate environment for making money.

This process is also an indication of why few senior managers in large trading rooms today, especially in larger institutions, were themselves great traders. In some ways, this is a good thing, because warrior traders are not always good people managers. The problem is that great people managers rarely make great traders or attain a true understanding of this noble pursuit.

The solution is for institutions to look more at the long-term performance of traders and less at their arguments, or lack thereof, for their positions. If someone makes a consistently good economic argument, perhaps he or she should be an economist or salesperson; however, if traders produce consistent losses, they should certainly not be traders, regardless of the quality of their arguments.

Good traders should also not be asked to offer an opinion on markets. This creates an environment where traders are socially exposed, meaning that their egos may begin to interfere with the normal flow of warrior trading. It is astounding how difficult management can find it to simply leave winning traders alone to do their own winning thing.

Ultimately, warrior trading is about an inner search and learning to trust in one's own ability. This allows traders to develop an internal freedom that enables them to focus on action. *Discussion* of markets can be endless and entertaining; however, it is only precise and consistent *action* in the market that delivers financial reward.

# CHAPTER 10

# CHOOSE YOUR WEAPON

# THE TRADING MATRIX

Moving from theory to practical application in any market is no easy matter, and the ability to do so is certainly not something to be taken for granted. So many market participants do a great deal of theoretical work on the market, spending time on how to determine the direction of the market and thinking that this is what trading is about. However, all they have done is develop a theory or their view—they have only completed the first step of a challenging and never-ending educational process. Seemingly oblivious, these market participants see their task as a finite and complete one, and they launch themselves into the battlefield completely unaware.

The market is a matrix where an enormous variety of issues can arise, some always present, some brief but intense in character. On top of this complexity, even those ever present issues that seem straightforward can wax or wane in terms of market interest, seemingly on a whim. In this environment, we must not only apply our theoretical view, but also remain personally objective and nimble.

## It Gets Personal

One thing that remains constant throughout your trading career is that it is always you as an individual who is participating in the market. It is the quality of your own interaction with the market that will have a bearing on your trading profits that is equally as significant as having the correct view on a particular market or

> *One thing that remains constant throughout your trading career is that it is always you as an individual who is participating in the market.*

stock. Therefore, it is important to remain objective, even when you are experiencing disappointment, and approach markets with a fresh perspective each and every day.

Success in trading is not just about markets and their direction. Rather, like any other modern business, it is really about your individual style of interaction with the market.

There is no single correct way to make money in the markets—there are about 6 billion ways to do so. In other words, there is a different way for every person on the planet. To achieve sustained profits and generate significant wealth, it is important to find your own way. While there are broad approaches and styles that can act as guides to profiting from markets, each individual must determine what works best for himself or herself. There is only one right answer for you, and no one else can tell you what it is. This right answer is the approach that fits you perfectly—this is the only approach you will enjoy and be able to stick to, profit from, and feel fulfilled by. Find the right approach—that is, in sporting terms, your unique swing—and you are assured of creating exceptional wealth. This can undoubtedly make things more complicated; however, given that the odds are heavily stacked against accumulating tremendous wealth, warrior traders commit to seeking out their perfect way. This is easy to say, but getting there is quite a journey.

## Finding Your Way

If you apply a style of trading that is in harmony with your own personality and objectives, success will abound. Everyone is good at something they love doing. Find your unique swing in any endeavor and you will have found your purpose, your love. It follows that if you develop your skill at trading in markets in a way that is comfortable and natural to you, you will be able to apply yourself in a consistent and winning fashion. From my experience, it is usually a lack of consistency that undoes many traders (even the great ones). A winning methodology is only such if it is applied consistently. If a method doesn't feel like your approach to markets and if you do not have a sense of owning the approach, you are unlikely to be able to stick with it—especially given the blows you are likely to suffer and the chaos you will witness on the actual battlefield of trading.

## RANGE WARRIORS AND TREND WARRIORS

To help you embark on the journey toward finding your own winning style, let's map out the terrain. Essentially, there are two different types of situations in all markets where opportunities exist for traders. They are *range trading* and *trend trading*. Most people are only comfortable doing one or the other—few people are happy doing both. Warrior traders should spend as much time as necessary to determine which approach best suits them and their lifestyle.

### Range Warriors

Range trading is for traders who enjoy buying things when they are cheap and selling them when they are expensive. If you are naturally a range trader, it is likely you responded to this statement by saying, "Is there any other way?"

If you look at stock market charts, it should become apparent that stocks tend to range for around 85 percent of the time—that is, they move between discernible channels of support and resistance. However, it is still important to realize that the price action within the range will become more random at times. This means it is paramount that range traders possess automatic and quick reflexes. Range, or day, traders will also be very active.

## Trend Warriors

Trend trading, on the other hand, is for people who like to be involved with the big events. Trend traders like to buy into an already rising market and keep the position for quite a long time.

Markets are trending—that is, covering large distances in relatively short periods of time—for approximately 15 percent of the time. The trend trader requires a high degree of patience coupled with the ability to constantly observe the market in a high state of readiness.

## What Type of Trader Are You?

To help you determine what style of trading would best suit you, some word association guidelines have been provided in Table 10.1.

You should also take into account your lifestyle and your resources in terms of both money and time. Range traders need to watch a market very frequently, if not constantly. Trend traders can look at a market once a day as long as they are disciplined about leaving orders with their brokers (in case the market starts to move without their knowing). Because range traders tend to do more frequent and smaller trades, their financial commitment may not be as great as that of trend traders, who can usually suffer some significant losses before capturing a big trend.

In the end, it comes down to what feels right to you—only you can know which is the more attractive to your unique self. Once you have decided on your style and perfected it, you can claim

**TABLE 10.1**   Determining Your Style of Trading

| Range Trader |
| --- |
| Characteristics:<br>Left-brained; practical and methodical; steady builder of wealth; buys cheap and sells when a profit is seen; strong work ethic; not interested in the forest, just the trees; has trouble dealing with losses, believes nobody went broke taking a profit. |
| **Trend Trader** |
| Characteristics:<br>Right-brained; creative and artistic; looking for a huge lift in wealth; does not really care what the price is when buying as long as it's going up; strong performance ethic; can see only the forest; losses are not important as big profits are coming; believes if you are on to a good thing, stick with it. |

the title of range trader or trend trader. You become a *warrior* when you learn to effortlessly express all the other knowledge of a warrior through your chosen style.

## ARCHERS AND SWORDSMEN

The mechanism for attaining the further status of warrior is either as a swordsman, if a range trader, or an archer, if a trend trader.

### Swordsmen

The way of the swordsman is akin to that of the range trader. The swordsman participates in the most immediate way, where constant movements of varying forms—such as thrust (trade), evade (take a loss), and the death blow (closing of the profitable trade)—are a continuous blur. Movement and reaction are so fast that the rational mind is almost eclipsed and the decision required at such speed is almost subconscious.

129

Typically, the futures pit (the floor of a futures-trading exchange) is the very physical place where the ultimate swordsmen compete. In this environment of furious action, the top pit traders often find they depend on a form of intuition, heightened to a reflex and referred to as "gut feeling." What makes great pit traders is their willingness to give in and commit to gut feeling.

Going with your gut feeling is not as easy as it sounds, especially if you are educated and knowledgeable. Perhaps this is why many a great pit trader is a streetwise person with little formal education. Formally educated people can be at a disadvantage in the pit simply because they have been bombarded with reductionist philosophy techniques for years.

While futures markets may be the environment where the action is so intense as to demand ultimate discipline, confidence, and technique, warrior traders can be found in every market.

The holistic approach to life suggested by Eastern philosophy was also followed by ancient swordsmen. After crafting a weapon and refining a fighting style, swordsmen enter a conflict in an almost unconscious and forgetful state. I don't mean unconscious in the sense of being asleep or knocked out; rather, I mean being not overly self-conscious and not relying on deductive or rational reasoning in order to interpret everything. After developing the independent aspects of battle, such as weapons and technique, swordsmen then call on something else and allow an innate process of action without thought to take over. Only in this way do swordsmen remain fast enough to sustain constant and rapid victories over their enemies and remain standing at the end of the battle.

> *After developing the independent aspects of battle such as weapons and technique, swordsmen then call on something else and allow an innate process of action without thought to take over.*

130

This is what many swordsmen traders have felt on entering and exiting their best trades, their biggest wins. They are often the least logical, yet the warrior feels in some way compelled to act—to sell or to buy. At other times, the warrior aggressively attacks the market in a most committed way. The point is that warrior trading, to a significant degree, requires traders to let go and listen to their intuition or gut feeling and to act in ways that may be different from the usual or logically thought-out plan.

## Archers

Archers are similar to trend traders. They cover the big picture from a distant observation post that allows them a clear view of the overall battle not afforded to swordsmen.

Archers act less frequently than swordsmen but do so equally decisively. Archers have a limited amount of ammunition, and it takes time to reload; therefore, they must use the arrow when it will be most effective. Similarly, trend traders, in attempting to capture large market moves, must avoid the usual volatility by having wider stop limits. This means that trend traders can lose their investment through a fewer number of trades than is the case for swordsmen. It is important for the archer to be out of the market as much as possible during nontrending periods.

In the markets, swordsmen are active for the larger part of the battle—approximately 85 percent. Archers are active for perhaps only 15 percent of the battle, but the archer's input can be as decisive as that of the swordsman. (As already highlighted, markets tend to consolidate for 85 percent of the time and trend for 15 percent of the time.) Both the swordsman and the archer participate in the same conflict and can subsequently get in each other's way, causing confusion for brief moments. However, both have the instinct and ability to assess the situation and withdraw or persist. Consideration of this point is beneficial to both archers and swordsmen.

While the secret behind the success of swordsmen is to be constant, the secret for the archer is to identify and choose the time of attack and the timing of the release of the shot. Don't be fooled, however; archers must be in a constant state of readiness as they wait for that right moment. The ultimate warrior archer also, of course, lets go of conscious involvement to the point where the shot "releases itself."

This ability—and believe me, it will take a long time and a lot of effort to attain—should be the goal of all trend traders. Great trend traders can, on occasion, almost "feel" a trend even before it has begun. Warrior archers will respond with lightning speed to confirmation as it unfolds on the battlefield, in terms of actual price action, because such development has usually already been considered in advance. Many other trend traders, those would-be archers, will have missed the opportunity. They have had to take aim clumsily, instead of having been in position with a sense of knowing, as was the case for the warrior.

This is the task of the warrior: to know what your target is going to do even before the target itself does. This has been a component of the art of war for countless centuries, and it is no less the case in modern markets. In understanding your quarry and how they think, the goal is always to maintain an accurate perception of the terrain so as to grasp the likely unfolding of events. This allows one to be in position ahead of time, as either an archer or a swordsman.

# CHAPTER 11

# BATTLE TACTICS

## THE WARRIOR TRADER'S ADVANTAGE

As a speculator, the only advantage lies in the ability to choose one's moment of attack—that is what I used to think. Now I know that there are many more advantages. The world has changed, and markets have evolved.

One of the biggest changes has been the advent of superannuation and hedge funds that now cast long shadows over the money markets. Some of these organizations have single traders who make the decisions on what to buy and sell and when. By far the majority, however, make investment decisions at committee meetings. This makes them conservative, slow, and, ultimately, part of the herd. The nimble speculator, especially the warrior trader, can easily outmaneuver such organizations, which creates a great advantage. The large capital flows in and out of markets are slow to turn, allowing plenty of opportunity for the warrior trader to be the first—to be in front of the wave of either buying or selling, whatever the case may be.

The other big advantage for the modern warrior trader is the huge leap that technology has made in the last 5 to 10 years. It was once a disadvantage being an individual trader because of the time lag that existed between when news and economic results were released and when individuals would get that news. Today, however, the news is instantaneously available to all parties, big or small.

Technology has also improved everyone's ability to access

markets. As with information accessibility, larger organizations at one time had better and more efficient access to the market itself. While this may still be the case for some of the new "hot" stock floats that periodically occur, usually all potential participants now have equal access. Included in this improved access is the reduced cost of trading. Using Internet-based dealing systems, individuals can now trade in most markets in the world immediately and at very low cost. Gone are the days of 1 percent or higher brokerage fees.

In essence, these developments have leveled the playing field for everyone. While warrior traders do have the advantages of choosing the moment of attack and being more nimble and better able to respond quickly to developments than large institutions, they now also have access to the same level of market news and information as quickly and enjoy the same low cost of trading. Most of all, the individual speculator is best positioned to pursue something very special indeed: the attainment of warrior trader status—that is, the perfection of the art of trading. Once achieved, given the other relative factors, the warrior trader can only grow stronger and more successful as time goes by.

> *. . . warrior traders do have the advantages of choosing the moment of attack and being more nimble and better able to respond quickly to developments than large institutions . . .*

So if you are prepared to take up the sword or bow (as the case may be), you can compete very effectively with the largest of players. David can indeed (and frequently does) slay Goliath. It really is just a question of skill, as the warrior trader can triumph over all other market participants, regardless of size.

## Choosing the Moment of Attack

Choosing the moment of attack is still an essential element of success. All great warrior traders enter the battle at just the right time, after having calculated this moment based on fundamental forces and events, technical price action, and the strength of their own and opposing forces. The right moment is likely to be a very brief window in time indeed. If one is focused elsewhere, the opportunity will be lost. If one recognizes the opportunity but is not in the correct state of mind, errors will be made. Thus, to be fully focused and in a perfect state of readiness at all times is to engage in warrior trading and, ultimately, to accumulate a vast fortune. (Assuming, of course, that your weapons and technique are up to speed.)

The first rule of conflict, then, is to enter the fray—and appear on the battlefield in the first place—only if absorbed in that perfect state of readiness. The second rule of conflict is that once the fray has been entered, the mind must remain still and ready for perfect action at any moment, without consideration or necessary consultation.

What this means in the real world of trading screens and financial activity is to have readied your weapons—that is, have prepared your economic and technical analysis, or whatever your particular weapons may be—and trained long and hard and thought through and tested your trading approach. Only then can you walk onto the battlefield and stand steadfast, waiting for the proper moment to arise.

Warriors know that they cannot control the battle but that they can move decisively as the battle evolves. Warrior trading involves constant participation. Often, actually having or not having a position is not nearly as important as your level of focus and attention and your sense of participation. If you are on the battlefield, your focus and your state of mind must be the same regardless of whether you have or do not have a position, and regardless of whether you are losing or winning. The state of mind, the openness to action, must remain constant.

The most common error in trading that I have witnessed is traders' enthusiasm becoming heightened once they have actually entered the fighting arena. All great battles have been won by the timely application of different forces and skills. If you are an archer, there is a time that is right for your participation. If you are a swordsman, there is another time when it will be most effective for you to use your particular skills. It is important that traders not lose this awareness in the initial excitement of entering the fray.

The following section examines what I consider the warrior trader's eight steps of battle, which will support you in your journey to total victory.

## THE EIGHT STEPS OF BATTLE

The eight steps of battle are intended as a guide to the new trader and a reminder to the experienced.

Perhaps the most important step is the last one. This step is simply to start anew once a position has been closed. It is important to understand that the last trade no longer matters—except in its potential to provide new knowledge. The emotional content of the last trade must be allowed to slide away. Once a trade has been completed, warrior traders must reflect momentarily and then start anew. On occasion, they must stand back and, from above the fray, completely reassess the status and nature of the market in terms of the big picture.

*. . . the last trade no longer matters— except in its potential to provide new knowledge.*

A common error of the average market participant, especially after a winning trade, is to charge ahead with the same idea and even greater enthusiasm. This often results in all the participant's hard-earned profits being returned to the market. Instead, traders must apply fresh thinking and proceed through each of the eight steps of battle after every trade.

The eight steps of battle encapsulate, albeit in brief form, the ongoing process of the warrior trader. This very same process may unfold fully in mere seconds for the swordsman, while for the archer, it may take place over several days or even weeks. There are 6 billion ways to make money in the markets—one unique way for each of us—but it is the application of this warrior process that supports and allows that unique swing to fully manifest itself and remain effective indefinitely.

## 1. Your Warrior Style Is Your Strength

Are you an archer, buying high and selling higher? Or are you a swordsman, buying low and selling high? It is important to distinguish between the two. To the swordsman, the archer is a fool who buys when the price is expensive. To the archer, the swordsman is risking all to buy into a falling market. These are simply different approaches. They are two sides of the same coin, with the coin being a combination of courage and conviction.

Do not be drawn into debates about which approach is best—either can work when applied by a willing and appropriate practitioner. You should, by now, know which style is better suited to you, that of the archer or that of the swordsman. Remain aware of this strength and avoid straying into an unsuitable style.

To attempt to play both roles, to be both swordsman and archer, is to make the mistake of trying to get the market right all the time—in trends and during nontrend consolidation periods. Such a strategy courts disaster. Each approach requires a different way of thinking and acting and, in effect, a different personality. Unless you have a split personality and can switch between them at will, it is best to choose your style—find your unique swing—and stick with it. Develop this natural strength, and focus it toward total victory.

## 2. Know the Terrain

What do you think is the true nature of the current and likely fundamental reality? What are your reliable and newly discovered real-world economists or analysts—that is, those who are capable of seeing the world differently—saying? Create your personal view, your image, of what is really going on in relation to your target market. Next, does opportunity exist based on your view of the fundamental reality? If so, what is the value of this opportunity? Does the broad market have the same idea and view, or is there evidence of an opportune fundamental variance between the market consensus and its reality? Find the immense opportunity that is lurking just beneath the surface.

Technically, you may be able to identify both a conservative wide range and a more aggressive narrow range of opinion within the consensus as your experience develops. Which you choose to take advantage of is partially a function of just how active you want to be in the market. For archers, however, it will probably be more profitable to be patient and wait for the best opportunities. The willingness to let your enemy draw closer, and so attain greater accuracy before releasing the shot, usually means fewer arrows are required. Courage and patience combined deliver greater accuracy.

Further, remember that all information is of value. The wider the spectrum of information that is considered, the greater the probability of success. The terrain of any market includes the long-term charts, which offer clues as to how fast a particular market can run and how long it usually consolidates before again embarking on a fresh trend. This can prove to be of tremendous value. Further, the short-term charts—not just their depiction of support and resistance but also their appearance and whether they show chaotic or clear patterns—are vital to the swordsman. The feeling for a market, or an enemy, that can be obtained from relative-strength indices and moving averages is equally vital. In effect, all this information provides warrior traders with something like a video simulation of their enemy's likely battle tactics. The information gained enables warrior traders, in the final battle, to outmaneuver and dominate their opponents.

## 3. Prepare Your Forces

Now that you can recognize in advance the real fundamental pressures and the significant price range, you can decide on your trading orders. Unfortunately, this sounds easier than it actually is. Even choosing your trading levels can take some courage. Having done your homework, however, you should be able to sweep any fear or self-doubt aside. Allow all the information to gel for a bit. By this I mean that after completing your homework, perhaps take a walk or do something else to allow your subconscious mind time to assess everything and distill it simply to either a buy or a sell order and to where that order will be positioned.

When I worked for a major global investment bank, the hardest message to get across to my colleagues was that I did my best work when I was out of the skyscraper and walking. You can imagine how well that went down with my workaholic colleagues who believed you should be seen at your desk at least 16 hours a day. But it was while I was out walking that I would get moments of inspiration that would allow me to sit back down at that desk, be courageously emphatic about a view, and decisively execute the necessary trades. Those same flashes of inspiration would then give me the courage and determination to do nothing as the profits increased. (Something I have learned through experience is that inactivity when on a winning trade perhaps utilizes more reserves of courage than any other aspect of trading.)

Once you have identified what the key technical price range is for you, and subsequently the important range break levels in either direction, it is time to place your orders. Archers will leave appropriate "enter position on stop" basis orders with accompanying "if done" stop-loss orders. (In other words, if warrior archers wanted to play a round of golf, they would first leave orders to buy a price range break to the upside. This would get them a long—bought—position in a rising market. To protect against a sharp reversal, they would need to then have a new stop-loss sell order, which is what the "if done" order would achieve. This way, when they get back from golf, they will have either a small loss or a big win. The point is, they will not have missed the opportunity they were looking for because they were at golf. Their warrior genius was working for them, even when they weren't glued to a screen.)

Warriors would never leave an order to enter a position without simultaneously leaving the associated stop-loss order. A secret agent might endorse a similar strategy: Never enter a room without knowing how to get out of it in a hurry.

Swordsmen will leave orders to buy on a dip where the stock is cheap that is just inside the range above the identified support level. They will be looking to take profit and go short the market toward the top of that range. The swordsman's stop-loss order will be just outside the immediate range and, hence, quite close to the position entry point.

Archers may also want to leave orders that go with the consensus view and against their own view. This can be done so as to capture any further opportunities that are still to come because of the "herding through the gate" effect, in line with consensus expectations. If archers are bullish, they can still be hitting profitable, though smaller, targets on the way down. This helps archers to stay in tune with and maintain a feel for the market, and to be involved even if it is going against their view. Just in case they were wrong, it also helps archers avoid watching a bear trend seemingly forever, while waiting for the favored bullish break. And there is nothing wrong with making money through a reverse strategy when you are wrong on your market view.

## 4. The Attack

Shrouded in the cloak of their enemy, or seemingly uninterested and nonchalant—so sit the warriors. These are the mastery manners of warrior traders in wait. Despite the surface appearance, however, the level of alertness, concentration, and focus is always high; it never wavers. It is no easy matter to remain in this alert state of mind for extended periods, poised in a constant state of readiness, waiting for the moment of sheer expression when the warrior joins the battle.

Being ready and in place for the coming battle by setting your orders well in advance provides a significant advantage. Do not wait—as many do, playing idle games on the sidelines—only to have to waste time reaching for and readying your sword or bow and so lose the moment when the precise alignment is right. Be already in place. This is paramount.

> *Being ready and in place for the coming battle by setting your orders well in advance provides a significant advantage.*

Modern trading procedures and systems allow you to do this simply by leaving orders in the market in advance. Warrior traders avail themselves of such facilities, for they provide them with the added advantage of being the first to strike at the level of the order. The order gives them speed.

Patience is the key. Once you have set your orders, you must be able to wait for the market to tell you when the moment is right. Wait for the market—that is, the battle—to generate the action; don't force it.

The actual attack should be the simplest and cleanest part of the whole process. There should be no thinking, deliberation, or consideration involved. All that has been done in preparation. The attack is clean, clinical, and sudden—it decapitates your nearest opponents in a flash, before they even knew you were there.

## 5. Stand and Fight

Standing and fighting is the truly hard work. You are on the battlefield now, and there is a frenzy of emotions besetting you—
pain, fear, ecstasy, greed, and sheer exhilaration and excitement.
If this is the case, don't even bother turning around. Just know
you are about to be decapitated from behind.

Those emotions have no place on the battlefield. If you are in
the market for the momentary thrill of experiencing such emotions, by all means stick around—as long
as you also enjoy writing checks to warrior traders as fast as you can.

*To be in the thick of
things with the market
(the battle) sometimes
running your way and
sometimes not is the
pinnacle of the
warrior's art.*

To be in the thick of things with the
market (the battle) sometimes running
your way and sometimes not is the pinnacle of the warrior's art. To be in play and,
whatever the situation—whether profits
are dwindling before your eyes or even if
losses are mounting, or whether profits
are accelerating—to remain unemotional and stick to your battle plan, is truly a skill that few seem capable of. However, I
would argue that all are capable of it. It is just that so few traders
stumble across the path to becoming warrior traders.

There can be a very thin line between being labeled a determined hero and being called a stubborn fool. It usually comes
down to the outcome, in the eyes of most people. For warrior
traders, however, it comes down to their willingness to be unemotional about the outcome or the progress of a trade and to always
be prepared to see things simply as a learning experience. Stand
and fight with a clear mind and trust in your ability to achieve
your objectives, all the time maintaining your exit options in a
disciplined manner.

Regarding exit points, however, it is important not to be too
focused on your stop loss—for where you look is usually where

you go (as any racing car driver will tell you). Look at and focus on where the battle is and where you expect it to go. If your stop loss is hit and you make a tactical retreat from the market for a period, it should happen in the blink of an eye. As a warrior trader, you should instantly enter a state of reflection and learning for a moment, before readying again for battle.

Once mastered, the stand-and-fight phase can be the most rewarding and satisfying aspect of warrior trading as you enter a blissful, Zen-like mental state. However, it cannot be achieved without all the other components.

## 6. Losing Ground—Enemy Penetration of Your Lines

Identifying price ranges of key consolidation periods is immensely valuable whether you have been forced to act defensively or you are going forward in attack. It is crucial to survival to identify in advance whether your view might be wrong and to determine what price level, when broken, would be in support of the consensus view. It is important to have a clear signal for when the forces rallied against the real fundamentals are too great (or perhaps for an occasion when you were simply wrong). This may be a temporary phenomenon—for example, a last gasp by the herd in the wrong direction. Whether you are right or wrong, and whether you are going to win the overall battle or not, the focus on any skirmish should be total.

Knowing these key technical levels in advance, you can prepare yourself for the likelihood of suffering some momentary losses after a line is broken against you and psychologically prepare yourself for a further rapid movement against you to the next stronger line. In effect, you are building up your ability to defend the occasional probes against you. The last thing you want is to be psyched out of a position just when the herd was about to exhaust itself. When an enemy is cornered, it will often fight with all its might for its one last chance at freedom. As a warrior trader, you need to be aware of this likelihood and pre-pare for it. If you can understand the nature of the incursions against your own lines in real time, you will also be able to take advantage of the opportunity provided for counterattack.

Try to also develop a feel for how everyone in the battle is thinking. In other words, know not just your own forces but the enemy as well. The market can be driven by the enemy (or the herd) for a significant period. However, once the enemy reaches exhaustion, it will then snap back in a major way in response to the real fundamental pressures you have previously identified. Until the enemy reaches that exhaustion point, though, it is still a force to be reckoned with. If the enemy is charging at the gates, patience is paramount. In every campaign, you will experience counterattacks by the enemy—expect them, plan for them, and, most important, be psychologically prepared for them.

Courage is about holding your course even when things are going against you. The usual representation of courage is that of the hero charging forward into the face of a fierce battle. While this can be courageous if it has been well planned, we most often need our bravery and our courage when things appear to be going wrong.

### Formidable Opposition

There are occasions when even warrior traders can run up against a formidable force. It can feel a little like someone has just walked onto the battlefield with a new form of technology—such as when the machine gun or even the tank was first introduced. Once again, however, fully aware and freethinking warriors can quickly ascertain and respond to this development.

The warrior response is to first withdraw and observe from a safe position. In this way, the warrior takes a moment to identify the Achilles heel of the new enemy weapon and to plan and execute an effective method to win the battle in spite of this new force.

For example, this situation might arise if you had been bearish a particular stock and then there was a takeover offer regarding it. Immediately taking profits on your short positions, you can then quickly assess whether the buyer will actually add value and reverse the bearish fundamentals that were originally driving your view.

A similar process occurs in foreign exchange markets where a central bank may try to keep its own currency weak by intervening and selling its own currency so as to enhance the nation's export performance. The central bank in such circumstances will, of course, argue that it is acting in accordance with the fundamentals, but are they the real fundamentals? If they are, the central bank will be successful in influencing the market and turning the tide. If not, as has been the case for the Bank of Japan for much of the last decade, they will lose, and lose badly, as their lines of defense are overwhelmed by warrior traders.

*When a formidable force that the whole market has become aware of is, in fact, fighting a losing battle, the eventual price movement—or the breaking through of the formidable barrier—will be extreme.*

Warrior traders hunt for such opportunities. When a formidable force that the whole market has become aware of is, in fact, fighting a losing battle, the eventual price movement—or the breaking through of the formidable barrier—will be extreme. This will force price action to travel large distances almost immediately, meaning vast fortunes can be made in a flash.

When George Soros was attacking the sterling—selling it aggressively and knowing that the Bank of England was buying—I was also selling sterling, though at much smaller volumes than Soros. It was as if the scent of blood was in the air—central bank blood, the blood of a formidable foe. The larger the beast that is attacked, the greater the variety of traders who will follow. The warrior traders are selling before the battle line is won, for they

147

sense that it will be. After the formidable opposition has been dispatched, the scavengers flock in and deliver further substantial profits to the warriors.

The same process has recurred throughout the history of markets, and in every market it will continue indefinitely. When a formidable force suddenly appears on the battlefield, take heart, for it represents a great trading opportunity. After reassessment of the fundamental picture, you may decide to run with the beast. Remember, however—the beast will win if it is in line with the fundamentals. Therefore, you know the worst-case scenario for that market and can go the other way with a good deal of commitment. Should you feel that the formidable force has it wrong and that in the end they will lose, all you have to do is choose your moment for victorious counterattack.

The price action surrounding such events as the entry of formidable forces that have got it wrong is almost identical on every occasion. The first sighting of the beast has your own forces scattering to the hills for cover. Then, with occasional skirmishes against the beast gradually increasing in duration and intensity, and as confidence builds, the beast's end finally approaches. On the chart, you will see the first flurry as a sharp spike away from the beast. Then there will be a slow, hesitant movement toward the beast. Another savaging, and the market again retreats from the beast—but in a telltale way, this flurry is not as agitated as the first. There may be five to seven of these flurries away from the beast, but each and every one diminishes in degree until the market is sitting on the beast. The collapse of the beast at this point is imminent. In a flash, the beast vanishes and is obliterated, and the market collapses with force— total victory to the warrior trader.

### Feigning Defeat
Stopping out of a position may give the appearance of defeat, but it is not meant to necessarily signal total defeat. While others

may see it that way, you must never be fooled. Stopping out of losing positions is the only sure way to maintain survival in difficult conflicts and to achieve the complete victory that is your aim. To learn how to live to fight another day is the best advice that all traders can be given. Not only is it the smart thing to do, but in the long run, the prevention of injury will act as a major building block of total victory. The warrior trader retreats not just to fight another day, but to fight a better day.

### Guerrilla Warfare

When seemingly in retreat, there is often a niche opportunity that will open up. If they have been long in a bull market and get stopped out on a reaction, warrior traders will often immediately place a fresh buy-on-stop order in the direction of their view just above the current consolidation. In this way, if they have been tricked out of their positions by a momentary thrust from the enemy, as the enemy then withdraws it will set off the traps the warriors have left. The warriors' stop-buy orders will accelerate the move back up, making it increasingly difficult for the opposition to get out of its short position. Warriors' flexibility works in their favor. They are immediately in profit on their latest trade and are back in the original position they wanted—that is, being long. The moral of this story, then, is when in retreat, don't forget to set your traps behind the enemy lines.

*When seemingly in retreat, there is often a niche opportunity that will open up.*

### Sending in Spies

While the archer waits for the perfect moment, the more active swordsmen may disguise themselves and fight with the herd for a period. As mentioned, archers can do this on occasion also, but they have to be more careful, given the finite nature of arrows as opposed to the indestructible, "keep trading" nature of swords.

Trading with the herd is simply a momentary attitude of going with the flow—a central tenet of the warrior trader's philosophy. The warrior trader may feel the market should be going up; however, after breaching the first lines of defense, the market continues to run south, taking out the last lines of defense and triggering the warrior's stop loss. As well as immediately placing traps behind the advancing enemy, warriors may on occasion hide themselves in the cloak of the enemy. The warriors realize that there could be money in being wrong if the herd still has further to run to the downside. Thus, the warriors go short the market that they still believe to be a bull market. In this way, warrior swordsmen have gained both strength and an intimate understanding of the herd that they are about to defeat.

Being part of the herd, warrior swordsmen will sense even more quickly the precise moment when the herd reaches its exhaustion point and can most easily be turned and defeated. This is a sophisticated level of warrior trading—the swordsmen cannot be emotionally or psychologically affected by their short-term position, nor can they lose their clear vision of an eventual bullish outcome while being short.

## 7. Taking and Holding Territory

### *Advancing through Enemy Lines*

What are the signs that show you are winning the battle and the enemy is on the run? While your own fundamental view may be either bullish or bearish, confirmation may be gained from the breach of whatever resistance or support level would represent a significant range break in support of your view. This is where you blend warrior fundamental and technical analysis to create a dominating force.

For example, a trailing stop loss can be aggressively tightened to the midpoint of the previous range should a front-page event occur for your market. Further, the effective combining of fundamental events, widespread media assertion of a trend, and technical analysis can lead to rapid advancement and securing of strategic benchmarks by locking in even greater profit levels.

Everyone has their own idea about trailing stop-loss orders (whereby a stop-loss order is gradually raised as the market continues to rally), but the suggested method for archers is to place the stop approximately 2 percent beyond the previous consolidation phase. For swordsmen, the margin will be significantly tighter, and each must determine this margin of his or her own accord, making this process a very active one indeed. During it, swordsmen will be in a high-speed state of intuition. While applying a trailing stop for a few moments, swordsmen must be fully prepared to take profit at the slightest inkling of a hesitation in price action, as this could mark a turn into an enemy response or possible market reversal.

For swordsmen, the stop-loss margin may vary with market conditions and the "feeling" for each trade. In the early stages of refining your art, however, you should seek to have a consistent stop-loss amount. This will teach you discipline as well as keep you sufficiently capitalized should you be wounded repeatedly. Remember: It is vital to still be able to fight the next battle.

*The magnitude of the stop-loss gap will vary for both archers and swordsmen and from market to market, and even with shifts in volatility. It is important to have done your homework.*

The magnitude of the stop-loss gap will vary for both archers and swordsmen and from market to market, and even with shifts in volatility. It is important to have done your homework. The stop-loss order can be moved up in the direction of the trend each time there is a fresh range break in that direction. This method constantly increases the profit level while avoiding most short-term corrections. The added bonus is the alleviation of the stress of wondering when to get back into a trend when profits have been taken too early. This anxiety can set off a debilitating series of blows. The loss of warrior trader harmony and the frantic attempt to find it again, instead of completely withdrawing for a period, can cause more damage to one's own forces than anything else.

We all lose step from time to time. When this happens, you must stand aside and let that battle pass. Regain your warrior state of mind and in true warrior fashion crouch in watchful awareness as you wait for the next trade to flow through you. Once you start to force the attack, you are destined for a significant loss. A trailing stop loss keeps you in the war, keeps you in tune with the war, and, most important, leaves you in full readiness to instantly strike again.

## 8. R & R

If this sounds like a wheel turning full circle, congratulations—it most certainly is. Like the wheel of a war chariot, you must be able to roll through the fiercest battles on a continual, smooth, and victorious path. It is this never-ending ability to "go" again and again—but in a balanced and calm warrior state of mind—that will lead you to the capture of every major market movement, without exception. Sounds good, doesn't it? It is.

Should you hesitate because of a series of losses, this hesitation will cause you to miss the large price movement that you had been seeking. You will have paid the ticket for your journey of advancing wealth, but missed the boat. You can maintain the perfect state of readiness for the perfect opportunity only through constant warrior awareness. You can be in that state relentlessly and yet comfortably only if you do not suffer serious injury. The disciplined application of stop losses will afford you this great strength. When people talk about stop losses, they do so from the financial or mathematical point of view. It is important to note that the psychological benefits are perhaps far more valuable. Stop losses keep you in shape in more ways than one. They keep the war wheel turning.

You do indeed need to be starting every single trade fresh and alert without any baggage from the previous encounter—regardless of whether it was good or bad. It is vital to start all over again and take a fresh look at everything—the fundamentals, technical analysis, market positioning, and consensus upon the countenance of each and every trade. Even in the quick cut and thrust of range trading and pit trading, this eighth step remains crucial. To start again with a fresh view after each trade is the way of the warrior.

# CHAPTER 12

# TOTAL VICTORY

**W**hat is *total victory*? It is quite an absolute term. Yet it is achievable in the real world. Warrior traders experience total victory because they live in a place of total victory.

Warrior traders are victorious even in defeat because they are already absorbing the experience, learning the lessons contained therein, and envisioning how they will be applied in the next battle and every battle thereafter. In other words, true warrior traders are wiser and stronger from the very moment of experiencing a setback or defeat. To warrior traders, all of their market encounters are another step forward—they are part of the total victory process.

Yes, total victory is a process—an ongoing process where wins increasingly outnumber losses, and the quantum of wins increases and the quantum of losses diminishes. The profitability is constantly being refined—not just in terms of quantity but also in terms of its very nature, in other words, the quality of the battle.

It is this ongoing process, the continuous journey, that so excites warrior traders. Warrior traders recognize that total victory is not a specific point—other than a point of reference within themselves. Total victory is not achieved after making your first million dollars in the market. Total victory is not achieved after a long string of profits. It is not achieved even after buying your first Ferrari or a tropical island. All of these things can be lost if you do not maintain a strong warrior trader mind-set at all times.

*Warrior traders recognize that total victory is not a specific point—other than a point of reference within themselves.*

Being a warrior trader means maintaining an inner strength and an outer ongoing trail of victory whereby profit performance constantly advances. It means reaching a point where a certain peace of mind is attained. At this point, warrior traders know that, regardless of any surprise attack from the enemy or any unforeseen battle defeat, ongoing success and victory are assured. The ultimate trick, the ultimate stroke of genius and wisdom, is to know that, through your own effort and state of mind, you are assured of success, and to not let this sublime awareness alter that winning state of mind in any way at all.

It is usually, and perhaps even always, the case that total defeat comes just as one feels total victory is in the bag. I mentioned the name Ferrari, and I have heard some warrior traders refer to the term *Ferrari trade*. This is when the trader has been having a good run and feels suddenly that now is the moment that he or she knows everything about this market, that now is the moment to win big—this is the day, the trade, that will mean tomorrow will be spent shopping for a Ferrari. This is what life is about and, due to the trader's great wisdom, he or she is now about to make a fortune.

Inevitably, this is the day this trader has one of his or her biggest losses.

## A CAUTIONARY TALE

The same pattern can unfold on a grand scale. I know of a high-profile currency trader for a major corporation who achieved spectacular profits in his first year of trading. The profits were indeed spectacular because the size of the positions was way out of proportion to those required by the company for its real business purposes. At this point, in my view, it was already a situation waiting to go bad—this fresh trader had experienced a winning streak with rather large positions on the order of hundreds of millions of dollars. Sadly, it is a pattern often repeated.

Starting with large wins usually leads a nonwarrior astray rather quickly. On this occasion, the managing director of the company is widely understood to have offered the young novice trader a huge financial reward should he or she produce the same results the following year. In fact, the company itself was struggling to make a profit and may well have recorded a loss that year if it had not been for the young currency trader.

Offering such rewards is probably the worst thing that can be done to a young trader. We were all young once, and if we look back, we can probably all acknowledge that we could be a little excitable about the prospect of making a fortune quickly.

In this particular case, the young trader had already convinced himself that he was one of the few smart people in the world when it came to currency markets—and to be fair, his only experience to date had been of winning. It never occurred to him that it might just have been plain luck when the market went the way he thought it would, and that the real reasons for that market trend were completely misunderstood by him. Such, I suggest, was indeed the situation. When the market reversed and began to behave differently—as is the experience of all those who believe they can control the market—it was beyond his comprehension. He had no real understanding of what was driving the market.

As the market went against him, according to his previous view it simply made a better trade, so he added to his now losing position. The forces he had always focused on as the driving forces of the previous year had not altered at all. The presumption in his mind, no doubt, was that "this approach worked for me last year, and this year it will work for me again." Still, on some level, I am sure all this young trader could see before his eyes the whole time he was trading was that island he intended to buy.

On and on the process continued. One would think it would have come to an end as the company decided it could no longer stand the losses accumulated. This was not the case. The losses grew beyond any reasonable level. At this stage, several banks started talking to each other behind the scenes about the losses at company Z. Most of the banks opted to sell their positions with the company—in other words, they swapped the positions into another bank's books at a small cost, just to get out of the situation that everyone else seemed to clearly understand was going bad. As for the bank that was taking on the losing positions in this company, it knew they were losses but it also thought that the company must have known what it was doing. Of course, the bank had no real idea how bad things were until it was too late.

There were no robust, independent reporting structures within the company. The board took its understanding of their foreign exchange positions largely from the young dealer. Given the losses, which ran into the many tens of millions, it is little wonder that the young trader had trouble breaking the news to his superiors. In any case, this young trader was a classic example of a trader who refused to learn from his losses. He viewed the market as less intelligent than himself, meaning it was only a matter of time before the market went where he "knew" it would go.

Finally, the bank that was left holding all the losing positions had to approach the board and say "no more." The bank wanted the losing positions closed and its money returned, thank you very much. The board was stunned and, of course, blamed the young trader completely. He was even labeled a "rogue trader" (as they all are). Yet, anyone placed in a position of immense responsibility without the necessary training and experience or associated independent reporting structure, and without appropriate managerial guidance, is going to end up being the main character in a cautionary tale of what not to do. Management did not support its trader with appropriate reporting structures and even spurred him on to greater and greater levels of risk.

Ultimately, it is not only the financial loss that hurts, but also the heightened sense of frustration. For the young trader, it was, no doubt, the disappointment of having been so close to a personal goal and then being sent further back from his objective that made him even more unwilling to admit his mistakes. This is a learning experience. More exactly, it is an opportunity to learn. We all pay large sums by way of losses for a fantastic education. But like any classroom situation, it is usually the case that just a few individuals are really paying attention, really learning. Most think they already know it all.

*The lessons are there for anyone, but few seem able to admit that they can learn more, that they can adapt their behavior to produce different and better results.*

The lessons are there for anyone, but few seem able to admit that they can learn more, that they can adapt their behavior to produce different and better results. Very few traders seem able to honestly, and with an open mind, examine the experience and their precise role in that experience.

## LOOKING AT PAST ERRORS

Here is the trick of learning in the markets. After a loss, warrior traders examine the market behavior, the price action, and the fundamental forces that drove the market in a different way from that which was expected. So far, so good, but warrior traders also examine their own thinking and the emotions they had that played a role in their defeat on this occasion. Were they greedy? Were they fearful? Were they complacent? To my mind, complacency is the greatest sin of all in the markets. No other error generates the immediate and significant losses that complacency produces.

These are errors of attack, but there are also errors of defense. Failure to set the stop loss wide enough is an example of lack of commitment. Were you trying to make a lot of money without being committed? Were you skimping on the price of the ticket to enter the arena? In warrior terms, did you fail to commit sufficient forces to get the job done?

The ultimate strength of warrior traders is their ability to invest their forces at the right time at the right place of battle. But you must be committed. Complacency can lead equally to an error of attack or one of defense. An example of an error of attack would be to employ too great a trading position in order to allow for the usual stop-loss margin for that trade. An error of defense would be to set a very tight stop loss, believing you were about to have an easy victory. They may sound the same, but there are subtle differences between these two scenarios.

> *In the end, it comes down to the determination of the individual to maintain the warrior code at all times. Constant learning, constant refining, constant humility, and total commitment are required.*

In the end, it comes down to the determination of the individual to maintain the warrior code at all times. Constant learning, constant refining, constant humility, and total commitment are required.

The lesson for warrior traders is to not become too excited about early wins. If you do so, you will sabotage any chance of total victory. Keeping everything in perspective is easier said than done, but it is precisely what you must do. It is also vital at all times to have a realistic understanding of the strength of your own forces. What is your bottom-line profit and loss situation? What is the balance of your trading account? Should you proceed with caution or aggression?

162

The correct answer is, of course, the same in all situations. You should proceed as a warrior trader, with caution and aggression perfectly balanced at all times.

In *The Art of War*, Sun-tzu suggests that one should seek victory only after the battle has been won. What is unique about trading, and what warrior traders come to understand finally, is that the battle is, at its core, with oneself. And this personal battle is won only through the experience of battle itself, through the constant refining of one's approach. In this ongoing state of total victory, immense fortunes can be made.

Total victory is, then, continuous victory—regardless of whether a particular individual battle was won or lost. Total victory is the winning of the war, and the war is never-ending.

# CONCLUSION

The core truth suggested here is that the consensus economic view of the world is often flawed and is of low correlation to real outcomes. It is this consensus-reality variance that generates the tremendous power of market movements and delivers warrior traders the opportunity to triumph.

The less traveled and more difficult path of seeking the reality over consensus—in combination with attaining an understanding of your personal style, or your unique swing—is the path to sustainable fortune.

Successful trading in markets is the result of striving for the real fundamental perspective and interacting with the market in a way that is comfortable for you. It is therefore sustainable in the long run, notwithstanding periods of error.

Irrefutably, we trade in a new market era. Economic fundamentals drive the major trends, but you cannot beat technical analysis as a provider of a road map to the swings and roundabouts that are part and parcel of every modern market. It is the simpler forms of technical analysis that are the most reliable and provide the most useful tools. When combined with an open mind, they enable the current pattern of behavior of a market to be perceived—another unique advantage.

Trading in markets is an exciting journey to be relentlessly undertaken, as long as it is constantly recognized and accepted as an evolving process and a never-ending learning experience. Approached with personal harmony and the application of a trading style that fits your personality, the journey of trading in markets can be both fulfilling and financially rewarding.

Market success may be more about you and less about the market than you first thought. Success is always about the level and quality of your interaction.

*Trading in markets is an exciting journey to be relentlessly undertaken, as long as it is constantly recognized and accepted as an evolving process and a never-ending learning experience.*

## THE SIMULTANEOUS JOURNEYS

The outer voyage is the attaining of a high level of understanding of market behavior. This requires education, study, and rigorous trading systems. Against this, the inner voyage is one of hard-edged honesty and self-examination, understanding, and to some degree, completion. At a certain point the two paths meet, and the circle is complete. This marks the birth of a great warrior.

Successful trading is about finding, controlling, and enacting your own style of interaction with the market. You must choose your weapon. You must focus and then work to develop your own methods of engagement, using the very specific and select set of weapons that you have chosen and that are in harmony with who you are.

This book is aimed at accelerating your understanding of how the enemy thinks and behaves, buys and sells. It should also clarify for you that the trading journey is as much a journey of personal development and exploration as it is about market fundamentals and hard-nosed economics. Yes, of course, you need to understand the mechanics of the stock exchange, such as what a share is, how options are traded, and where things like indices come into play, but it is important to realize that having knowledge of such simple facts does not guarantee success as a trader. Practically every trader in the market understands the simple facts of market trading and the rudimentary logistics of buying and selling shares and other financial instruments on the exchange. What separates the successful trader from the break-even bunch and the bankrupt majority is true understanding. It is a trained mind-set, an orchestrated art, that acts with a singular purpose: to profit from trading.

In brief, success at trading in markets comes about by shifting from an attitude of being the *observed* to becoming the active *observer*. By doing so, you will come to sit on the mountaintop, seeing the lay of the battlefield and the way it will likely unfold in advance of the vast array of combatants huddled in the valley. This allows you to act with a timeliness and rapidity of action that ensures a victorious and safe homecoming, time and time again. This is a crucial step toward becoming a warrior trader.

Making the initial decision to trade on the stock exchange is often exhilarating and may indeed propel you into a whirlwind education from which you can acquire the rudimentary tools of trading. But if you think this decision will automatically lead to a profitable and prosperous future, you are sadly mistaken. The real choice you, as a trader, must make is whether you are happy to enjoy the rewards of participation, in much the same way as one would enjoy participation as a spectator at a sporting event, or whether you truly desire to be among the few who are the beneficiaries of tremendous financial wealth.

The question is, are you willing to enter the realm of the warrior trader? Are you ready to maximize the immense opportunity of financial markets, in a warrior state of mind, while trading with the weapon of choice? Being a warrior is, as it always has been, hard work. It offers amazing rewards and is all for the noble good. Whether you enter the realm of the warrior really isn't up to the market. It really is simply up to you.

The secret of warrior trading is to have courage in the context of constant learning.

# INDEX

Disasters, effect on market,
  19–20
Dot-com bubble, lessons from,
  116, 119

Economic theory:
  failings of, 12–19
  lagging the markets, 22–26
  and market analysis, 5–11
  and patterns of human behav-
    ior, 12–17
  versus reality, 15, 19–22
Economists:
  consensus forecasting, 79–82
  as market predictors, 8–10,
    17–19
  performance of, 107–108
Elliott wave theory:
  versus author's trend analysis,
    44
  caveat, 31
  continuation patterns and, 46
Emotions, human. *See* Behavior,
    human
Energy theory, market, 63–66
Euro, collapse of, 85–86
Euromoney Foreign Exchange
    Conference (London), xvii
Exhaustion phase, market, 41–42

Fear:
  as market driver, 44–46, 57–58
  profiting from, 91
Federal Reserve, U.S., 5–6
Ferrari trade, defined, 158
Financial markets. *See* Currency
    markets; Foreign exchange
    markets
Forecasting, market:
  by consensus, 79–86
  and economic theory, 6–11
  reductionist theory and, 12–16

technical analysis and, 29–30,
    36–38
Foreign exchange markets:
  Australian dollar, 83–84
  author's career path, xv–xviii
  economic engineering and,
    147
  euro, 85–86
  role of speculation in, 71
Front-page effect, 20–22
Fundamental analysis. *See*
    Analysis, fundamental
Fundamental shift rate (FSR),
    38–39, 44
Futures pits, stress of, 114, 130
FxMax advisory firm, xvii, 8

Global currency markets. *See*
    Foreign exchange markets
Governments, influence on mar-
    kets, 54–56
Greed:
  as market driver, 44–46,
    57–58
  profiting from, 91
Greenspan, Alan, 5–6

Herd mentality, 72–75
  and contrarian trading,
    108–110
  profiting from, 94–95
  versus warrior mentality, xi–xv,
    107–112

Impulsive waves, 45–46
Information and energy theory,
    63–66
Information technology, effect on
    trading, 135–136
Interest rates:
  impact on currency, 83
  impact on market, 16